THE RAMPART

For Kay,
I love you so much!
Blessings on you!
          Vanessa Chavez

VANESSA CHAVEZ

WESTBOW
PRESS®
A DIVISION OF THOMAS NELSON
& ZONDERVAN

Copyright © 2015 Vanessa Chavez.

All rights reserved. No part of this book may be used or reproduced by any means, graphic, electronic, or mechanical, including photocopying, recording, taping or by any information storage retrieval system without the written permission of the author except in the case of brief quotations embodied in critical articles and reviews.

This book is a work of non-fiction. Unless otherwise noted, the author and the publisher make no explicit guarantees as to the accuracy of the information contained in this book and in some cases, names of people and places have been altered to protect their privacy.

Scripture taken from the New King James Version. Copyright © 1979, 1980, 1982 by Thomas Nelson, Inc. Used by permission. All rights reserved.

Author Photo: Portraits by Tracy

WestBow Press books may be ordered through booksellers or by contacting:

WestBow Press
A Division of Thomas Nelson & Zondervan
1663 Liberty Drive
Bloomington, IN 47403
www.westbowpress.com
1 (866) 928-1240

Because of the dynamic nature of the Internet, any web addresses or links contained in this book may have changed since publication and may no longer be valid. The views expressed in this work are solely those of the author and do not necessarily reflect the views of the publisher, and the publisher hereby disclaims any responsibility for them.

Any people depicted in stock imagery provided by Thinkstock are models, and such images are being used for illustrative purposes only. Certain stock imagery © Thinkstock.

ISBN: 978-1-5127-2348-9 (sc)
ISBN: 978-1-5127-2349-6 (hc)
ISBN: 978-1-5127-2347-2 (e)

Library of Congress Control Number: 2015920513

Print information available on the last page.

WestBow Press rev. date: 12/14/2015

I dedicate this book to my precious girls, Miyah and Maddy Kate. My prayer is that I live my life in such a way that teaches you to see God's indescribable love and beauty always at work in you and through you. May you always hear His sweet voice as He whispers your name. May you know Him as the One you can trust in your celebrations as well as your disappointments. May you realize your value and give your all, to fulfill your God-breathed dreams.

And to my husband, David, where would I be without you? You make every day a delight. Without your love and encouragement, I would be incomplete. It is out of our three-strand cord that God's love and ministry freely flows. I love living life with you.

Acknowledgments

To Jesus, my Savior, Rescuer, Healer, Redeemer, and Friend. Thank You for leaving the ninety-nine to rescue me. Thank You for taking the unlovely and fashioning something breathtaking. Thank You for allowing me the honor to be a carrier of Your life, love, and hope.

To my favorite everything, my husband, David, for being the wind in my sails. Thank you for your prayers and for believing in me and the bigness of our God. Your love, leadership, and selflessness have opened wide the doors for God to pour His love out.

To Pastor Stan, for giving of your time and expertise to sharpen me and my writing. Thank you for being a precious portion of the blessing God has poured out upon our family.

To my Nana, mom, and sisters, for believing with me. Thank you, Melissa J. Wilkins, for creating the amazing cover for my dream come true. Thank you, Nana, for all the tea parties and coloring dates you had with my sweet little darlings to give me moments of uninterrupted time - to do a little writing.

Contents

Introduction xi
Chapter 1: The Wait 1
Chapter 2: The Deal 17
Chapter 3: The View 32
Chapter 4: The Dream 47
Chapter 5: The Rod 58
Chapter 6: The Season 69
Chapter 7: The Octagon 81
Chapter 8: The Cloud 94
Chapter 9: The Plunder 109
Conclusion 123
Notes 125

Introduction

Rampart? That's a word I'd expect to find on the top corner of my morning newspaper as the "word of the day," a word I've never seen before and would have to turn to page 4a to discover its meaning. My first encounter with this word was in Habakkuk 2:1: "I will stand my watch, and set myself on the rampart, and watch to see what He will say to me, and what I will answer when I am corrected."

I was intrigued by this man admitting to God that they weren't seeing eye to eye. I remember a conversation I had with a friend while driving to church one Wednesday evening during our late teen years. We were arguing over whether it was okay to be angry with God. She was convinced that just as we could be mad at our Earthly fathers, we could be mad at our Heavenly Father. I was convinced it was a serious sin to be mad at God, because He was God and never did anything wrong. Not long after that theological debate, God in His gracious manner showed me how wrong I was.

It's inevitable that humanity will journey through life and not fully understand God and His ways because His ways are far above ours. Isaiah 55:9 tells us, "For as the heavens are higher than the earth, So are My ways higher than your ways, And My thoughts than your thoughts." But still, our natural tendency is to rely on our thoughts to lead us and decipher the truth we live by day to day.

So what are we supposed to do when we don't see eye to eye with the Creator of the universe? The moment their ways differ from God's, some people distance themselves from and maybe even part ways with God for a time. Others ignore the nagging questions and stuff them away somewhere deep down. But Habakkuk refused to remain in that place where his soul couldn't trust God. He refused to grow numb or complacent. Instead, he chose to get alone and climb.

Habakkuk climbed onto his rampart and waited with full expectation that his God was going to show up and meet with him face-to-face. He refused to climb down until God fixed everything that was now broken.

You can probably recall a time when you had to wait for God; maybe you are still waiting. You wait for a heartfelt prayer to be answered; you wait for a promise to be fulfilled; you wait for Him to show up; you wait for Him to explain "why." Regardless of why or how long you wait, there is much to overcome in the stillness.

In my own times of wrestling with not understanding "How could God ...?" or "Why would God ...?" or simply "Where is God?" I have learned He is who He says He is even when it doesn't seem so. Life is full of trials; we live in a broken world, and our trials can be used for good if we allow God to walk with us in the midst of our heartaches.

As I have felt His leading to share some of the tools He has revealed to me in my times of questioning and waiting. I hope you're encouraged as you journey through your own waiting and wondering. I'm still learning much, and I've come to know I'll never fully understand God and His ways. At times, I'll find my heart once again struggling to move forward with Him throughout difficult seasons. But as He revealed to me the difficult, painful, beautiful place of *The Rampart*, I'm compelled to share it with you.

My prayer is that you are encouraged in whatever season you now find yourself. And if He is calling you to climb upon your rampart, I pray you'll be infused with courage to meet Him face to face to see what He will say to you.

Chapter One

The Wait

It is doubtful whether God can bless a man greatly until he has hurt him deeply.
—A. W. Tozer[1]

O Lord, how long must I call for help before you will listen? I shout to you in vain; there is no answer. "Help! Murder!" I cry, but no one comes to save. Must I forever see this sin and sadness all around me? Wherever I look I see oppression and bribery and men who love to argue and to fight. The law is not enforced, and there is no justice given in the courts, for the wicked far outnumber the righteous, and bribes and trickery prevail. (Habakkuk 1:2–4 TLB)[2]

Scholars think the book of Habakkuk was written around 612 BC, though the view from his front door doesn't sound much different from my own. I can't remember a time when the news pouring into my living room didn't contain brutal murders, deceitful leaders caught in the act, and billion-dollar scams that have stripped many of their life savings. The innocent suffer at the hand of the heartless, cities are devoured by vicious weather, and countries are devastated by natural disasters. Slavery is rampant all over the world, and millions go hungry.

Habakkuk was grieved over the sad state of his nation, and he was losing hope. The law no longer carried authority; violence, scandal, and strife were all around him. He cried out to God, for there was no one else big enough to intervene. But as God breathed out His answer, Habakkuk was left shocked and horrified. Betrayal was unleashed upon him. It was an answer that seemed to go against the very nature of who God was. Habakkuk had been overwhelmed by the devastated condition of his day, and the only glimpse of hope—of things turning around or at least hindered from growing worse—was God. He must have thought, *Surely God can do something to make it better. After all, God is the only true thing. He is the only One in our world who is supposed to be unchanging, dependable, loving, and big.*

God's answer was somewhat less than comforting to Habakkuk and his people. His answer to His son's cry for hope was the Chaldeans, who by God's description were "a bitter, impetuous nation" and a "terrible and dreadful people"(Habakkuk 1:5–11). God was "raising up" these vicious men to attack Habakkuk's people—God's chosen people. To our human understanding, that was heartless and unloving. His answer sounded like punishment; it was as if they'd made Him so angry He was going to pull out the paddle and let loose.

> For as the heavens are higher than the earth,
> So are My ways higher than your ways, And My
> thoughts than your thoughts.(Isaiah 55:9)

God recognized that the Judeans' hearts were so hardened and so set on self-destruction that if He allowed them to continue in their apathetic course, they would grow more set in their lost ways and potentially pass the point of no return. In His higher ways and His grace, love, and mercy, He was going to give the enemy free reign for a time to make the Judeans uncomfortable to the point that they would once again cry out to God and allow Him in to take care of them. This was no act of vengeance or anger; it was an act of love. If we heard God's words to Habakkuk, we would most likely feel this same betrayal. Many of us have felt betrayed by who He was supposed to be and His felt failure to be that.

God's answer to Habakkuk for hope would be like God answering our cries for America with a terrorist attack. In all his humanity, Habakkuk couldn't comprehend how his God could be so cruel. This answer seemed to go against the very nature of God and who His Word said He was. This brings us to the rampart. "I will stand my watch, And set myself on the rampart, And watch to see what He will say to me, And what I will answer when I am corrected" (Habakkuk 2:1).

Rampart is one of those words rarely used today, but it's a *"tall, thick stone or dirt wall that is built around a castle, or town to protect it from attack."*[3] Because the Bible wasn't written in English, much of the original meanings behind these words have been, as they say, "lost in translation." The original languages of the Bible used words that contained paragraphs of meaning. As I was reading Habakkuk's encounter with God and his struggle to trust his God, I turned to the Hebrew definitions of this passage. I have listed some of the terms used to define each word, but for the full terms and definitions, please refer to Biblesoft's *New Exhaustive Strong's Numbers and Concordance with Expanded Greek-Hebrew Dictionary.*[4]

> I will stand my watch And set myself on the rampart, And watch to see what He will say to me, And what I will answer when I am corrected. (Habakkuk 2:1)

- will stand: `amad; abide, continue, dwell, endure, establish, remain, tarry
- my watch: *mishmereth*; watch, the post, duty, charge, keep, safeguard
- set myself: *yatsab*; to place anything so as to stay, set self, remain
- the rampart: *matsowr*; something hemming in, a fastness, a siege, defense
- will watch: *tsaphah*; to lean forward, to peer into the distance, to wait for
- to see: *ra'ah*; to behold, discern, have experience, gaze, meet, perceive
- will say: *dabar*; to speak, answer, commune, declare, teach, subdue
- shall answer: *shuwb*; to turn back, fetch home again, reverse, set again
- am reproved: *towkechah*; chastened, correction, reasoning, rebuke

Putting it all together, this passage can be paraphrased like this: Habakkuk was going to establish himself on his post and refuse to leave his tower. While he waited, he would lean forward in anticipation. He would peer into the distance, waiting to gaze upon and experience God. He would wait confidently knowing that God would show up and fetch him home again.

Many people in Habakkuk's day built walls around their cities for protection. These walls had ramparts, or sniper towers, large enough for arrows to fit through but small enough to protect guards from incoming attacks. Ramparts were the place one would go to watch and wait for his enemy.

Just as ramparts were used to keep the enemy out of the heart of a city, Habakkuk realized in this area of his life, his soul perceived God as an enemy—one who wasn't safe to be let in. He knew that unless he met with God at the place where one goes to meet his enemies, he wouldn't be able to go any further with God; his faith and trust would be stopped there.

We have to be honest and bare all before Him. Many of us don't even know what that truth entails; we just know that the moment we feared God or felt betrayal or confused by Him, we immediately pushed these feelings into the closet of our hearts and locked the doors. We didn't dare let God know what we really thought. But He already knows even better than we do what we've locked away. Many of us ignore this; it's easier to become numb and quench all hope than to face the betrayal we feel. We stop. We don't know how to pray anymore because praying didn't work last time.

Many of us get busy walking circles in the wilderness and never entering our Promised Land. We don't believe it even exists anymore. The Israelites experienced this and voiced their lost hope to Moses: "For it would have been better for us to serve the Egyptians than that we should die in the wilderness" (Exodus 14:12). Serving the Egyptians meant hard labor, and many of the Israelites' friends and family members had been worked to death. These were the very people who killed babies during the time Moses was born, and this didn't happen to the Israelites forefathers; their own brothers, sons, nephews, and grandsons *were* the babies murdered under Pharaoh's command.

Many of us have heard this story and watched movies about the Exodus, but it easily becomes just another story with a villain. However, there was no way the people had forgotten the day Egyptian soldiers stormed into their homes, pried crying babies away from screaming mothers, and in sheer hardness of heart killed them before turning back to hit the next block. The Israelites were so disappointed that God hadn't shown up sooner with their Promised Land in the desert that they preferred to go back to being tortured by the Egyptians. They longed for torture and slavery over trusting God in the wilderness. God hadn't come through as they had expected He would.

Have you ever prayed a faith-packed prayer that went unanswered? The Bible says our prayers are powerful enough to move mountains.

> For assuredly, I say to you, whoever says to this mountain, "Be removed and be cast into the sea," and does not doubt in his heart, but believes that those things he says will be done, he will have whatever he says. Therefore I say to you, whatever things you ask when you pray, believe that you receive them, and you will have them. (Mark 11:23–24)

I've prayed many a prayer resulting in a growing mountain rather than one being cast aside.

The Bible says we can pray for it to rain upon our dry land and rain will pour.

> The effective, fervent prayer of a righteous man avails much. Elijah was a man with a nature like ours, and he prayed earnestly that it would not rain; and it did not rain on the land for three years and six months. And he prayed again, and the heaven gave rain, and the earth produced its fruit. (James 5:16–18)

I live in the Texas Panhandle; we suffer many dry days, and combined with our winds, the lack of rain often leads to devastating fires. It's common on any Sunday to hear a pastor lead a congregation in unified prayer for rain upon our land. And even with all those people gathered as one in prayer, we still suffer through months with zero precipitation.

The Bible says our prayers will save the sick, "And the prayer of faith will save the sick, and the Lord will raise him up" (James

5:14–15). I've lost precious people to sickness while wearing my knees out in prayer.

These truths can keep us from believing in the power of prayer or God's faithfulness to His Word. In trying times, our heads continue to tell us what we know the Word says, but our hearts cry out in hurt and disbelief, "It didn't work last time, so why should I expect it to this time?" If we're honest, we might admit that at times such experiences left us in anger and tears, questioning whether God really cares about us. Some in their suffering even question if there really is a God.

I can recall many times that my heart and head weren't in agreement. In the midst of a battle in which I couldn't see, hear, or feel God, my head was quick to remind me that He was always with me, but my heart couldn't comprehend His felt absence. The truth in our hearts is a truth, but it doesn't always line up with what we know as the truth in our heads.

We can't stay in this devastated stance. We are all children of God knit together in our mothers' wombs by our Creator. We weren't created by chance or accident. God didn't have a quota to meet the day He fashioned us; He intended to create us. He wanted to piece us together, weaving into our beings a purpose and a call.

> For You formed my inward parts; You covered me in my mother's womb. I will praise You, for I am fearfully and wonderfully made; Marvelous are Your works, And that my soul knows very well. My frame was not hidden from You, When I was made in secret, And skillfully wrought in the lowest parts of the earth. Your eyes saw my substance, being yet unformed. And in Your book they all were written, The days fashioned for me, When as yet there were none of them. (Psalm 139:13–16)

You have a piece of God's image that no one else has (Genesis 1:27). He's chosen you to do great and mighty things for His kingdom, and the world awaits your contribution. "For we are His workmanship, created in Christ Jesus for good works, which God prepared beforehand that we should walk in them" (Ephesians 2:9–10). If you remain in a place of untrust with God, those around you, people you know, and people you've yet to meet will miss out on the treasure you carry within. You'll miss out on being fulfilled in this world.

One day, I let Dakota, my boxer, out to run in the field behind our house. I'd never seen him run so fast and with such uncorked passion; I sensed in that moment complete fulfillment. He was born to run! There's nothing as satisfying as doing what you were born to do. If you have ever had the privilege of carrying out your passions, you know exactly what I'm describing.

So how do we move past this place with God? Only He can line up the truth in our heads and hearts with His Truth, but He doesn't expect us to do it without His help. It's not easy, and it requires much work. We're used to quick fixes, but God isn't interested in doing quick work; He knows what can come of the waiting.

> *My brethren, count it all joy when you fall into various trials, knowing that the testing of your faith produces patience. But let patience have its perfect work, that you may be perfect and complete, lacking nothing.* (James 1:2–5)

I'd love to be counted as one who is "perfect and complete, lacking nothing" by His standards and work. Habakkuk started by acknowledging that he couldn't understand or trust God. He put himself on his rampart with a resolve that he wasn't going to leave that place until God had met him and transformed his heart. He asked, "Why?" and he waited. Looking for God, he waited with expectancy as he "peered into the distance," searching the horizon. Is it a sin to question our Creator? Our heads tell us He's never wrong. The Word tells us He's always good: "The LORD is good to all, And His tender mercies are over all His works" (Psalm 145:9). But there are times when our hearts tell us He has abandoned us.

My favorite part of the crucifixion story is when Jesus in all His humanity cried out from the very depths of His soul, "Eli, Eli, lama sabachthani?" "My God, My God, why have you forsaken me?" (Matthew 27:46). I find it so easy to relate to Jesus as God. He healed the sick, turned water into wine, and raised the dead. But knowing Jesus as a man is hardly comprehendible. Most of us have no idea how God will turn our trials into good or why He allows us to cross through them, but Jesus knew exactly *why* He had to endure the cross. He wasn't asking His Father to lay out the plan of salvation for Him again; He knew in three days He would come out of that tomb. He told the guys several times that week it would happen. His head knew exactly what God had promised and what the Word said about His experience, but His human heart couldn't comprehend how a loving God, His own Daddy, could allow Him to suffer this.

Did Jesus sin by voicing the cries of His hurting heart and expressing His heart's betrayed state? No. He was without sin. What makes this even more precious is the fact that He didn't just whisper it in His prayer closet, He yelled it out for you and me and all future generations to hear. "I, in My humanity, don't understand you, God!" When He says He is not a God who doesn't understand our weaknesses, He means it. He knows what we're feeling better than anyone else.

> For we do not have a High Priest who cannot sympathize with our weaknesses, but was in all points tempted as we are, yet without sin. Let us therefore come boldly to the throne of grace, that

we may obtain mercy and find grace to help in time of need. (Hebrews 4:15–16)

So what does the waiting look like? Wouldn't we love an answer to this question? We'd know what to expect, how long we'd wait, and what it would look like when He finally shows up. But if you've spent any time walking out the Word, you know God isn't in the habit of being predictable. He's a personal Friend, and each of us walks a different path with Him. His foundational truths never vary, but each of us has a different encounter with Him as He teaches us who He is.

During one of my waiting times, I had a vision:

> *I was in a dark tunnel. The space was small, and the ground was made up of hot coals. As I looked down, I was shoeless. My feet were burning. I looked behind me and found no opening. I had been walking this ground for some time. In front of me there was a glimmer of light in a tiny, little puddle that had room enough for one foot at a time. I ran as best I could toward that puddle, tripping several times along the way. Each time my skin hit the coals, it burned away, revealing a golden light underneath. When I finally made it to the puddle, I dove in with all my heart. And as I did, the puddle grew. The relief was amazing. In that brief moment, pain and loneliness faded, and as I looked up, I saw Jesus mid-dive, coming to join me in my puddle. We giggled and splashed and played for what seemed hours. It had been a long time since I'd laughed. I didn't want that time to end, and as it did, I looked ahead and saw nothing but darkness and the dull glow of hot coals. No words were spoken, but I looked into His eyes, pleading with Him, Please don't make me do this. I didn't know what awaited me on*

the other side, but in my heart, I knew that there was another side and that our time together in the puddle had given me the strength I needed to make it there.

I understood that this tunnel experience had been a place He led me to walk. Even though I felt isolated, alone, confused—*What is this? Why is this?*—I understood I wasn't alone and wasn't being destroyed. What a clear picture of how His ways are higher than ours! He never leaves us; we're never alone no matter how alone we might feel.

This coal-walking experience was just for a time; there was an end to this tunnel. I could see the golden light breaking through my burning skin; this walk was somehow melting away my flesh and allowing a pure light to shine through me.

We won't always understand all the whys, but He will lead us and grace us to trust Him even when our questions remain unanswered.

How can we be faithful with the promises given to us in the Word? In July 2007, my husband and I were given the opportunity to walk this out. Our oldest daughter was eighteen months old, and because we had noticed some asymmetry in her back, we took her in to be examined. Her pediatrician immediately ordered X-rays determine if scoliosis was the diagnosis. I wasn't educated in reading X-rays, but it was very clear that her spine was in the shape of an S.

We were referred to an orthopedic surgeon for further treatment. He took additional X-rays that showed her curves were digressing rapidly. We were told her only hope was to put her under so the surgeon could fuse a metal rod to the top and bottom of her spine. She would have to undergo surgery every three months to extend the rod to keep up with her growing body. She would require ongoing back surgeries until she finished puberty. We researched these surgeries and learned of the many possible complications she might face.

To add to this difficult walk, the moment she was diagnosed, our insurance company rescinded her policy, which meant it was as if she had never had any insurance coverage. We began receiving bills for every well- check and doctor's appointment she'd had had since being covered by this company. We were also informed that she would no longer be eligible for insurance coverage of any kind.

During this same time, my husband worked in the auto industry. In the year preceding her diagnosis, America's economy began to plummet, and one of the hardest-hit areas was the auto industry. He was the finance manager for a Saturn store, and as his pay was 100 percent commission, his paychecks began dwindling.

That same year, my job also underwent some major changes. My employer walked into some tough times financially and wasn't sure he could continue to pay me. I ended up starting a new job, but that transition from my previous job had robbed a lot from me emotionally. And it wasn't long after my transition that GM announced it would no longer manufacture Saturns, and my husband's job of fourteen years closed its doors. He went four months without a paycheck, and that lands us right about the time we received our little one's diagnosis.

We began researching scoliosis. Everything we read left us feeling hopeless. We met with multiple chiropractors who informed us there was nothing they could do for scoliosis, especially in one so young with such large curves. We came across another option with a hospital in Dallas that treated children for free, but the treatment included casting her from neck to waist, which would inhibit her lung development and cause muscle atrophy. She would have to be recast every three months to accommodate her growth, and if the cast procedures weren't successful, she'd have to undergo the surgeries. Several professionals told us that if we didn't treat her soon, she'd begin to be in pain and her internal organs would be at risk of incurring damage.

We sought prayer, lots of it. We were given words that God was going to divinely heal her back. We looked up the verses in the Bible that promised God's healing, and we asked for divine wisdom in the decisions we needed to make. We prayed these verses; we battled in the spirit realm and made positive confession with our mouths.

I'd had just about decided to stop researching on the Internet as it only only hindered my faith, when my husband came across a new technology for non-surgical treatment. We made the call to these doctors in New York and found they had experience working with little ones and had already seen great results with their bracing treatment. We also found that they traveled to various offices around the nation to treat patients in other areas. We immediately scheduled an appointment to meet with them on their next trip to Texas.

Before we left for our first appointment, our church prayed over us and began standing in faith with us. We made the trip. When we got there, the doctor put the flexible brace on her and took the next set of X-rays. He was dumfounded. The X-rays showed her curves had improved; he looked confused. He told us he couldn't put her in the brace, but he did want to see her again in three months. He made it very clear that the amount of improvement with no corrective procedures wasn't normal, and we were quick to tell him that many prayers had been prayed.

We were ecstatic! We had no doubt God had worked a miracle; we knew "He who began a good work would be faithful to complete it" (Philippians 1:6). We testified the following Sunday morning and shared the incredible news with friends and family. We continued to read the verses on healing, make proclamations, and battle in spiritual warfare.

Before our first appointment, I made a brace for our daughter's favorite doll to look just like the one pictured online. Before our second appointment, I took it off as an act of faith that we wouldn't be needing it, and we made our next trip with full expectation of more improvement in her condition. However, the next set of

X-rays showed digression, and we left his office with our little baby in a brace.

I had to climb up on my rampart at that moment. She had to begin this journey, which started out with her falling flat on her face multiple times while her little body tried to adjust to this new posture and tension. We also had to tell all those who had heard the news from our first trip that God hadn't really come through as we thought He had.

Several of them were unbelievers, and the thought of contributing to their doubt in God and His faithfulness to His Word was heart wrenching. I had many tell me that if we'd had just had more faith, God would have been able to complete the healing. Others told me that there must have been sin in my life that had caused this to happen to my little girl. These words did not come from strangers.

I felt powerless in my prayers, and I knew in my heart there wasn't one ounce of doubt in my God's ability to heal my baby. I knew He could heal her at any moment with one word, one look, or one prayer in whatever way He wanted. He could have healed her. It felt as if He simply had chosen not to. I think the hardest part of this trial, aside from her walking it out, are the moments when she comes to me in tears wondering why her prayers aren't working.

I have to testify that God has made provision. We travel every three months to see the specialist, the fees and the brace were adding up especially when my husband was four months without a job. Of the then, twelve offices around the U.S., one of them just happened to be five minutes away from my mother's home in the Dallas area in her local chiropractor's office. If you've ever been to the Dallas/Fort Worth area, you know that getting anywhere in five minutes is unheard of; many commute over an hour just get to work every day. Her specialist is amazingly kid friendly; we love him; she loves him.

We also found a local chiropractor who wanted to work with her alongside the specialist's care, and he, knowing how expensive treatment would be, he began her treatment for free and blessed us even more by praying with us for her healing. He is also kid-friendly and loved by us. We were able to get insurance coverage for everything but scoliosis-related care. The brace, which we call her "super suit," has kept the curves from digressing; she hasn't had internal pain, and the biggest praise of all is that she hasn't had to undergo any surgeries! God hasn't failed us; He continues to be ever so present throughout our journey.

One of the ways to be faithful during your wait is to praise God for what He has done and is doing. We have a tendency to focus on what we don't have, and we thus neglect to recognize the ways He *is* moving in our lives. Our being faithful with what we have been given is to continue praying the promises He has given us in Scripture, to continue making positive confession with our mouths, and to testify of how He *has* provided for us.

God has whispered specific Scriptures into our hearts that we cling to. We even wrote one on her super suit: "I will go before you and make the crooked places straight" (Isaiah 45:2a). We also do physical therapy. This is how we are to be faithful as we wait.

Miyah is eight now, and we've never stopped believing for her divine healing. I trust that God's timing is perfect and beyond my intel. We've prayed from the very beginning that God would use our situation to impact people—our families and friends, the doctors, their families and patients, and their friends with our testimony of His powerful intervention. We know He promises in His Word to take what the enemy means for harm in our lives and turn it for good.

> *And we know that all things work together for good to those who love God, to those who are the called according to His purpose.* (Romans 8:28)

Regardless of why you find yourself waiting, these facts remain: Only you can climb up on your rampart. Only you can make yourself stay there until you encounter Him. And Only God can transform your heart.

Chapter Two

The Deal

> *Times of heartbreak will inevitably touch us all.*
> *But each of us must determine if we become*
> *broken or shattered. The first leaves us humbled*
> *before the throne of God and capable of being*
> *'poured out' to a hurting world. The second*
> *leaves us an embittered pile of worthless dust.*[1]
> —Jeanne Mayo, "Mom"

I was in the middle of a praise-and-worship service many years ago when I saw a vision of myself as a young girl having an encounter with God:

I was a young girl, clutching my doll and skipping along when God approached me. I could sense His joy in watching me like a parent taking delight in simply seeing His daughter just be little.

After a few moments passed, I sensed Him asking, *Who takes care of your heart?*

Without missing a skip, I casually answered, *I do.*

He wanted to make a deal with me and asked if I was interested in hearing more about it.

Sure, I replied midskip.

Smiling, He began to share the deal with me. I would never have to be alone again. I could have someone with me everywhere I went. My eyes lit up at the thought of having someone to talk to all the time.

He continued as He personally promised, *You'll always have the things you need. You'll never have to go without. You'll always be loved even when you mess up. You'll be able to sit on My lap anytime you want. You'll be kept safe from the bad guys. You'll receive amazing gifts picked out just for you.*

I contemplated the deal. *What do you want from me?* I asked, standing still.

All He wanted in return was for me to allow Him to be the Keeper of my heart and to trust Him to take good care of it.

It didn't sound like much of a trade; in my childhood mind, I thought it would be one less thing to have to keep up with, so what did I have to lose? And so I shook hands with my Creator to seal the deal.

Still clutching my doll with one hand, I took my heart in the other and held it out to God to make the exchange. I had the look of confidence on my face. I knew everything in my life was about to be great.

Just moments after my surrender, an enormous sledgehammer came crashing down on my exposed heart. I turned around expecting to find Satan's grip on that hammer only to discover God Himself had delivered the crushing blow.

Shocked and devastated, I grasped the broken pieces of my heart, dropped my doll, turned my back to Him, and walked away in search of someone to put my heart back together, but everything I tried only made things worse.

I couldn't tell how much time had passed before I approached God with my accusations. I demanded, *How could You be so cruel? I trusted You! You came to me! You offered the deal and You broke it!*

Have you ever felt that betrayal? You find yourself confused and hurt by the very One who was supposed to keep you safe. The wound can strike so deep that it renders you completely speechless, stunned, and without an ounce of desire to take your next breath. Maybe you haven't experienced His "hammer" to that intensity, but I believe all of us have had that moment, at least once, when we discovered He wasn't exactly who we believed Him to be and doesn't always do things the way we were sure He would.

For many of us, our question is not in what He did to us but why He didn't prevent things from happening to us. "If He's all powerful, why didn't He intervene? Why didn't He stop this bad experience from happening? Where was He when I needed Him most?"

This hammer experience immediately throws us into a war zone. Our hearts cry out in disbelief, and our feelings call into question everything we ever believed to be true about our Heavenly Father; we challenge and question every Sunday school lesson we've ever learned.

These attacks are launched at our minds, and our thoughts are flooded with doubt and unbelief. The very next bullet comes from the enemy, who has been waiting on crouched paws for this opportune time to bring back to our remembrance all the ways our God has supposedly failed us or our loved ones. The mind, bombarded by this onslaught, struggles to recall the Truth, but it seems so far out of reach.

In these moments, the very nature of who God is becomes challenged by our souls: *The Word says He is good.* "*The LORD is good to all, And His tender mercies are over all His works*" (*Psalm 145:9*). Would a truly good God allow such heartache in those He is supposed to love so much?

He did respond to my demand for an answer. In His bittersweet way, He revealed that He didn't break our covenant, I did. His part of the deal was to take my heart and begin His perfect work in me.

My part was to trust Him to take perfect care of me. As soon as He began His good work in me, I stopped trusting.

He showed me the true state of my surrender. My commitment to Him was actually, *God, I'll trust You completely as long as I understand what You are doing in me, but the moment You surpass my understanding I'll withdraw my trust from You.*

He showed me what I had walked away from. I stood, unable to find thoughts or words. He took what looked like a pile of sawdust, and with His huge hand, He mysteriously picked out a single piece. In one hand, He held a needle threaded with gold, and in the other, a tiny piece of what I could not tell. I had no sense of time as I watched; I was mesmerized by His precision. He carefully selected the next piece to be sewn into His handiwork. When He finished— tears graced both of our faces— for He held in His hand, a solid-gold heart.

He then whispered to me that He longed to transform my heart to make it look and flow like His own. The only way He could accomplish that was to crush my heart so He could rebuild it piece by piece until it was woven so tightly that nothing could pierce it. His work was pure, beyond any other. His desire was for me to be like Him. When my heart flowed like His, nothing could separate us and nothing could hinder His work through me.

Hosea put this whole process into words for us: "Come, and let us return to the LORD; For He has torn, but He will heal us; He has stricken, but He will bind us up" (Hosea 6:1).

When I looked at this verse in its original language, I was blown away. The Hebrew definition for "has torn" is "to pull or tear to pieces," and the definition for "will heal" is "to mend by stitching, and to make whole."[2] Isn't it amazing that the Creator desires to spend this kind of time with us? He could simply choose to not care if we ever grew beyond our self-centered state. He has enough angels and power and prestige to assign someone else to piece our hearts back together, yet He chooses to be the One to stitch by stitch rebuild us. He wants to be that close to us, and He doesn't trust anyone else to do it as perfectly as we deserve it to be done.

I don't use the word *deserve* lightly. We sinners deserve a bunch, but such loving, intimate attention isn't the first thing that comes to mind. We don't deserve His loving care because of what we've done; we deserve His love because of who we are, the "apple of His eye" (Zechariah 2:8).

I want my family to have the very best of everything this life offers. Since He loves us much more than we could ever imagine loving our own children, how much more does His heart yearn for us to have the best?

> *If you then, being evil, know how to give good gifts to your children, how much more will your Father who is in heaven give good things to those who ask Him!*
> (Matthew 7:11)

During one evening service, our congregation was singing a song proclaiming that God is worthy of our praise. I stood in the moment of that song questioning how my praise could be of any value to the King of Kings. He deserves the best, and praise from a human being doesn't seem worth much. I immediately sensed His heart; towards me - He had created me to simply be with Him.

His heart's desire is for us to love Him back with the love He gives us. Our praise is worth more to God than we can comprehend. The worship we pour out upon Him is a way we communicate our love, admiration, desire, and yearning for Him. He yearns for us.

Many of us began our journey as Christians with expectations not much different from those of the little child in this vision. Once we sacrificed our all to Him, He would then owe us a happy life without heartache. And since the King of Kings would adopt us, we would have a right to live a life of royalty. The problem is not in the belief that we are royalty, heirs to the throne of Heaven's Kingdom, this is true! No, the problem is in our expectation of how a Heavenly prince or princess should be treated in this world. Jesus told us what to expect; we just didn't get it.

> *And you will be hated by all for My name's sake. But he who endures to the end will be saved.* (Matthew 10:22–23)

The Israelites had expectations much like these. They had been told for generations that the Messiah would come as a mighty, powerful King. Jesus came into town riding on a borrowed donkey; He was then killed by men. If He truly was a King, where was His army? Many saw Him as weak and powerless. These walked away from that scene believing this man, Jesus, was not the Messiah; their Messiah had not yet come. But He did come. I wonder how many times we've walked out of a season in our lives believing that God didn't come when in reality He did come; He just didn't come in the way our natural minds expected to see Him.

It's in our nature to rely on our own thoughts and wisdom when it comes to making choices and assessing circumstances. Our natural minds cannot comprehend the ways of God, but He orchestrated it that way on purpose. He could have created us with the ability to think on a higher level, but He loves us too much for that, for He also knows that it's in our nature to be self-reliant. If we didn't have a need for Him, we would never seek Him. It's in our *need* that we're made fully aware of our lack and of His fullness. He did this not to reveal to us our lowliness and His greatness but to ensure that at least some of His beloved children would through their need meet Him as the One who can provide for our needs as well as the One who delights in doing so.

> *And He said to me, "My grace is sufficient for you, for My strength is made perfect in weakness."* (2 Corinthians 12:9)

There are many Sscriptures that warn us of a life of trial and tribulation, but the verses on God's faithfulness far outnumber the verses on trials. You and I are already aware that we face trials as our world grows scarier with each sunrise. The question then that resonates through many hearts is this, "Was this a 'good' God's plan and intention for my life? If He is loving and caring, how could He allow these horrible things to take place?" I've heard these questions come from people of all walks of life. I was grieved to hear one man's story of how he used to walk with God until he traveled the world and saw God's absence in the midst of hunger, natural disasters, and people ridden with disease. Has God abandoned us?

In my own quest for why God does what He does or doesn't do what He chooses not to do, He took me all the way back to the beginning of humanity. God's best plan for us was to be naked and unashamed living in the Garden of Eden (Genesis 2:25). Life there didn't include mortgages, grocery stores, gas pumps, divorce court, the White House, or the IRS. It was simply man and woman and God in paradise. Adam and Eve's daily to-do list consisted of hanging out together, naming animals, and deciding which of the many amazing fruits they were going to eat next. Can you imagine a life that simple? Most of us today can't stand to be still or in silence for more than a minute before we reach for our cell phones to drown out the quiet. We feel guilty when we sit down to rest. And, I'm amazed at how many of us today can't function without energy supplements, caffeine, and sleep aids.

God's best for us was a much simpler life. This was a life beyond our imaginations, but the best part came during the cool of the day: "And they heard the sound of the LORD God walking in the garden in the cool of the day" (Genesis 3:8a). Adam and Eve literally walked with God in the garden. That was His design for us—intimacy with Him and each other without shame, with nothing to hide; a life without stress. His purpose for creating us was for relationship. His definition of relationship looks nothing like our present-day verison. He wants us to know Him. The Hebrew word for *know* is *yada*, "to know by experiencing."³ He wants us to experience Him, and after a lifetime of experiencing Him, there will still be so many pieces of God we will have yet to *yada*. He intends to introduce Himself to us daily while we walk together.

His best for us also included a life without the knowledge of evil. This story in Genesis shows us the heart of our Heavenly Father and how He wanted to protect His own from tasting the fruit of that tree He knew would usher us all into a world of knowing and experiencing evil.

> The Lord God took the man and put him in the Garden of Eden to work it and take care of it. And the Lord God commanded the man, "You are free to eat from any tree in the garden; but you must not eat from the tree of the knowledge of good and evil, for when you eat from it you will certainly die." (Genesis 2:15–17)

In the beginning, the Creator gave man authority over the Earth. When you give someone something, it no longer belongs to you, and the one who receives your gift will decide what becomes of it. Your gift might be returned or exchanged; it might be re-gifted; maybe it will be enjoyed to its fullest or tucked away in a closet never to be used. God's gifts to us are no different. He even says in His Word that His gifts do not come with ultimatums, "For the gifts and the calling of God are irrevocable" (Romans 11:29–30). He doesn't give us things and then demand we use them or even that we use them a certain way. He is gracious enough to offer to teach us how to use them.

I have resorted to flipping through many a user's guide that was included with gifts I've received; some of the guides were very helpful, whereas others left me wondering if the writer of the guide had actually ever laid eyes on the item. The awesome thing about God's gifts is that He is the user guide and makes Himself available to us at any moment. Since He created our gifts, He knows the best way to use them.

Humanity received Earth as a gift. When Adam and Eve disobeyed, they brought sin and death upon it. The Earth and all creation were instantly cursed. They didn't take care of their gift. As God is faithful to His Word, Earth belonged to humanity, and only humanity could reclaim authority over it. Since God is holy, He cannot dwell with sin. God had to keep Adam and Eve out of the garden not because He was angry and felt they deserved to be punished; if they would have stayed in the garden, they might have eaten of the Tree of Life and forever be alive in their sinful state, leaving no hope for redemption (Genesis 3:22–24).

This cursed place in which we walk is not God's best for us, but He so desired to walk with us that He made another plan: "For since by man came death, by Man also came the resurrection of the dead. For as in Adam all die, even so in Christ all shall be made alive" (1 Corinthians 15:21–23). He knew before He even breathed life into Adam that he would choose sin and that Jesus would have to become man and die, yet He created Adam anyway. He was so desperate for relationship with us that He willingly paid the greatest price.

Now He leaves Heaven in all its splendor to walk with us in this cursed world. It is the cursed state of Earth that makes up our trials, not our loving Father. He is all-powerful; He allows things to happen in our lives but doesn't delight in them. He can use them for good if we allow Him to do so.

I was blessed beyond measure to be a youth minister right out of high school for about eight years. People would scoff and joke that my job consisted of video games and nachos. They had no idea the conversations that went on in my office, at the snow cone stand, or in the gym. My job was to walk with these kids in whatever life they lived. It would have been awesome if the weight on their shoulders were simply deciding which candy bar would go best with their weekly bowl of nachos. Many times I listened to these precious teens share heart wrenching stories of abuse, abortion, cutting, rape, divorce, identity struggles, or just missing their dads so badly they could barely cope. I knew I had only a brief moment to try to teach them how to cope with life, to deposit a drop of hope knowing they'd be leaving my office or Wednesday night service or café table and walking right back into a nightmare.

One teen came to my office every week, and I had an hour to sit with her and be a shoulder she could cry on. My job was to show up with sutures and bandages to stop her emotional bleeding. I stopped the bleeding and bandaged her up only to send her right back out onto the battlefield she called home. I knew that the next Wednesday, she would be right back in my office bleeding again. She was just one of hundreds I was blessed and charged to walk with in my time as a youth minister.

I can remember so clearly the one day she walked out, and I closed my door, drew the blinds, and cried out to God, "Why don't You intervene? Rescue her! Be Big! Just pick her up right now and take care of her?!" He reminded me of how He introduced Himself to me in each struggle; if He had rescued me before it was time, would I now know Him as my Healer, Daddy, Friend, Provider, Savior, Deliverer? I knew the answer. I was reminded of the many times I'd said that I wouldn't change my difficult life for an easy one, a tear-free one, because I met God through each struggle.

He reminded me of the vision He gave me of myself in a war-torn land. *I was standing alone on a battlefield, being attacked by multiple enemies wielding swords. Each blow cut right to my bone. I was defenseless. He reached down, picked me up, and sat me in His lap. He took His time with each wound. I winced at the burn of antiseptic being poured over each cut; it was almost unbearable, but He wiped every tear from my face and continued until I was completely clean, stitched, and bandaged.*

He put His armor on me, gave me a sword, taught me how to fight, and put me right back in the same spot He had rescued me from. Only that time, when the blows came, they bounced off my armor and didn't cut to my core. It was then that I was able to rain blows on my enemies.

God introduced Himself to me through my trials. I wouldn't know Him as Provider today if my family hadn't had to depend on Him every day to provide our next meal throughout my childhood. My mom and I have reminisced about the year we ate nothing but pinto beans. I have to say, I still love a good bowl of beans. I'm the oldest in my family, and all my clothes were given to me; my entire childhood wardrobe consisted of hand-me-downs that God provided. I can remember the one time I got to go school shopping. My best friend's mom took me to the store to pick out a shirt the day before I started eighth grade at a new school. I'm many years past eighth grade, but I can still picture that shirt in detail. Today, I never worry about going hungry because I know—I've experienced—God as my Provider.

I also know God as my Deliverer. When I was growing up, three of the six houses on my street housed pedophiles. Sexual abuse clothed me with shame, fear, addiction, and rejection. I know what it was like to be so bound up in shame that I believed everything I did was different from the way everyone else did things and that the way I did them was horribly wrong. I couldn't even use the bathroom in elementary school if anyone else was around; I avoided the water fountain and learned to hold it for hours.

I was always the last one to go to sleep at slumber parties because I was convinced I slept wrong. In first-grade choir, I remember lip-synching to every song because I just knew I sang wrong. Everything about me was wrong and worthy of rejecting. I had horrible nightmares almost every night. I lived in a constant state of fear, scared someone would discover how wrong I did things, and I was terrified of men.

I had been so rejected throughout my school years because we were poor that it only compounded the rejection I felt from being horribly wrong that I actually got to a place in seventh grade where I didn't talk to anyone ever. I answered with a yes or a no, and that was about enough to get me by.

I began to live in daydreams, my only safe place where I felt loved. Those closest to me know my favorite superhero is the Incredible Hulk, but what most of them don't know is that I used to imagine he lived right outside my bedroom window, keeping me safe from the bad guys. I became addicted to daydreaming. My God delivered me from all these things that the enemy would have used to destroy me. If my future had been destroyed, how many teenage lives would have gone untouched?

I also know God as my Healer. I had severe asthma well into my twenties. My doctor gave me a blow test that contained a red, yellow, and green zone. After blowing into it, if it got to the yellow zone, I was supposed to use my nebulizer. If it registered in the red zone, I was to go immediately to an urgent care facility. I lived in the red zone. Every time I blew, it would end up in the red. I'd use my nebulizer and get into the yellow for a few hours.

For years, I asked God to heal me. One weekend, I attended a women's retreat; the speaker gave a word that some of us had been asking God for miracles. She had us stand, and asked those around us to pray for us. I didn't share my miracle request with the woman who prayed with me, but after a few moments of our fervent prayer, she whispered in my ear that God was going to heal me. He gave me specific instructions on how to walk out that word of promise. My husband and I prayed, and we felt I was to stop all medication and pray through any asthma attack.

God has a unique way to heal and touch each of us, so I don't advise anyone to quit taking any medications based on another's testimony. But I prayed through each attack, and after some time, I was completely healed of asthma. On my twenty-fifth birthday, I was finally able to blow out my own candles on my birthday cake!

I met God as my Daddy. Growing up in a broken home left a lot of holes that only God could fill in my life. My heart had cracks of brokenness that ran so deep only the love of God was small enough yet also big enough to reach and fill.

The broken nature of our home left us all needing to encounter God as our Abba, Father. My parents divorced when I was in seventh grade, and I needed God desperately. The things the enemy had robbed me of were what drove me to God. He is my All in All.

At most of my friends' weddings, I watched the brides be led around the dance floor to the Bob Carlisle song "Butterfly Kisses" in their daddys' arms. I was blessed to have my brother walk me down the aisle, but there was no one to fill that special role of father to dance the father-daughter dance with me at my wedding. My mom has since remarried a wonderful man, but he came along as I was graduating high school and leaving home.

One evening, I sat on my bed and talked with God. I reminded Him that His Word said He was our All in All and would meet any need we had, and so I crawled into His lap as I'd done many times before and began to tell my Daddy all about this really amazing boy, my best friend, who had asked me to marry him. God really did fill this void in my heart, and to this day He is still my Daddy.

These experiences are what "qualified" me to be a youth pastor and walk with those teens. God wants to be there for us in every way. Our trials open up opportunity for Him to reveal who He is and longs to be in our lives. There's nothing easy about it, and it is a process that requires much work. What are you being qualified to do or become?

One night, we were holding a prophetic prayer time; teams of leaders spent time fasting and praying over a specific group of people asking the Lord to share a special word from His heart over them. As we were praying over our group, I knew I was to share the verse that says, "The Lord disciplines those He loves" (Hebrews 12:6a). This is not a word one gets excited about sharing, but in obedience I spoke it out, believing there would be more words of encouragement and clarity to share alongside it.

And as I began to share, these words flowed out of my mouth: "As an athlete disciplines his body through diet and exercise to prepare for his competition, the Lord places us in a boot camp of specific disciplines to prepare us for the race. He knows what awaits us, and just as a soldiers endure seasons of intense discipline to prepare them for the battle in which they will soon fight, our merciful Commander, puts us in training. He will never in His mercy, send us to fight in a war, we aren't first trained and equipped to win."

The training ground, however, is seldom seen for what it is. Many times in my life I looked with eyes of comparison upon those around me. I didn't understand why I felt I was constantly walking uphill in army boots with the Texas Panhandle wind blowing its seventy miles per hour in my face while those around me were riding in luxury cars sipping ice-cold beverage with the air-conditioner gently blowing their hair.

God doesn't call us to compare our lives with those of others; He was quick to remind me that He is in charge and can do whatever He pleases in my life and in the lives of those around me. He has a specific role for each of us to play in His plan, and each role requires different training.

One of the most inspiring stories I've been blessed to read is that of Corrie Ten Boom. She yielded to God and His Word regardless of the cost. Her training ground included many months in the Vught and Ravensbruck concentration camps during the Holocaust. Reflecting back upon her life years after her release, she said, "This is what the past is for! Every experience God gives us, every person He puts in our lives is the perfect preparation for a future that only He can see."[4]

He is good *all* the time, and His ways are beyond our understanding. He has a plan to use every trial this cursed world issues us for our good and for His glory. We have to trust Him even when He does something beyond our comprehension. When it's all said and done and we can look back on our lives, would we trade a few months of comfort for another's salvation or our own intimacy with the Creator?

Not every trial will be used to reach the lost, but He promises in His Word that every trial can be used to build character, to introduce us to a piece of God, and used to fashion and form us in His image so He can use us to make a difference. In whatever way He offers you His deal for your life, know He always has His best awaiting you.

Chapter Three

The View

> *Mountaintops are for views and inspiration,
> but fruit is grown in the valleys.*[1]
> —Billy Graham

I spent a few years waiting tables and loved it. I learned so much about people, including myself. While working at the Olive Garden we had specific jobs that had to be completed before we left each shift. The silverware had to be rolled, the floor hokeyd, and the salt and pepper shakers filled before we could clock out.

But there was one job required only for certain sections and was probably the least favorite task of all the servers. Certain sections had mirrors the width of the booths, and these were prime targets for messy little fingers to paint their works of art,; the medium of choice being salad dressing. To clean these mirrors in a way that would grant us permission to go home, we had to take our focus off of everything reflected in that mirror and focus solely on the spots on the surface of the glass. If you have ever had the opportunity to clean windows you can relate to this same *change of view*. I love the way Benjamin Warfield worded it.

A glass window stands before us. We raise our eyes and see the glass; we note its quality and observe its defects; we speculate on its composition. Or we look straight through it on the great prospect of land and sea and sky beyond.[2]

The Lord spoke clearly to me one morning about how my life was like a mirror. I can get so focused on one little spot on the surface of my life that I completely tune out anything beyond the glass that is being reflected in the mirror. There is so much more to life than the one circumstance, thought, or experience that can so easily consume us and captivate our attention, energy, and thoughts and these spots make up such a small portion of our lives.

Isn't it amazing how we can allow our focus on one mistake to drown out all of the other amazing things we reflect in our daily lives? Or maybe it is the one mistake we focus on in someone else's' life that hinders us from seeing all of the other amazing attributes they possess? By the same token, I have experienced times when God has taken me from being able to see only a tiny water spot on a window to seeing the grass, trees, flowers, birds, and clouds beyond the glass. He didn't move me or change my circumstances; He simply changed my perspective.

A simple change in perspective could be all we need to keep on keeping on during trying times. This shift can take us from being hopeless to being hope-filled. There will always be more than meets the eye for us while on Earth as there is a spirit realm that encompasses us and yet remains unseen by the natural eye.

I am always encouraged by reading Daniel's experience in Daniel 10. He was walking along the Tigris river with a group of men when he looked up and saw an incredible sight. But the those standing by him, looking up at the same sky, saw nothing. They were overcome with terror; they had a different view. An angel appeared and shared an incredible truth with him. Daniel had been fasting and praying for twenty-one days on his rampart, while Heaven remained silent. Many of us get discouraged after five minutes in our prayer closets; I've had my own moments of giving up, assuming the silence from up there had something to do with my lack of ability to pray the right way. At times, I've even assumed His silence was His way of saying no.

Daniel persisted and found that an angel had been sent to deliver him a message from the very throne room of Heaven on the first day he began to seek God's counsel; the twenty-one-day delay was solely due to spiritual warfare. How quickly we forget that we have an enemy who lives each day to keep us from God and the fulfillment of His plans for our lives. What would have happened if Daniel had given up prematurely? This entire story had to do with the destiny of a nation; Daniel's obedience to pray and wait impacted generations.

One of my favorite perspective changes took place in Dothan. As the king of Syria was preparing to attack Israel, Elisha, who was miles away from the king's chambers, heard from the Lord the enemy's plans and sent word of it to his king, the king of Israel. The Syrians, tired of being thwarted, suspected a spy in their ranks only to discover that is was a prophet of God who was continually exposing their plans. They sent a great army to Dothan to put an end to this "prophet" problem. Elisha and his servant awoke, stepped outside their tent, and were greeted by the view of an entire army waiting to take them. It was the two of them against the entire Syrian army. Elisha's servant couldn't help but voice his concern.

> Therefore he sent horses and chariots and a great army there, and they came by night and surrounded the city. And when the servant of the man of God arose early and went out, there was an army, surrounding the city with horses and chariots. And his servant said to him, "Alas, my master! What shall we do?" So he answered, "Do not fear, for those who are with us are more than

those who are with them." And Elisha prayed, and said, "LORD, I pray, open his eyes that he may see." Then the LORD opened the eyes of the young man, and he saw. And behold, the mountain was full of horses and chariots of fire all around Elisha. (2 Kings 6:14–17)

I'd love to get some Elisha goggles and walk about life "seeing" the armies of Heaven that surround and await to fight on my behalf for His glory.

The amazing thing about this story is that God didn't even use the mountain full of horses and chariots of fire to defeat the Syrians; He simply heeded Elisha's prayer and struck their entire army with blindness. They actually asked Elisha where to find Elisha, and he led them to Samaria, the very camp of their enemies.

How we limit our God. He waits for us to trust Him and invite Him into our overwhelming circumstances, and if we would just allow Him to direct our prayers and steps, what amazing stories we could share from our own experiences. No enemy will ever outnumber our God, He fears nothing and no one. If you are surrounded by an overwhelming view today, I pray your eyes be opened to see those with you far outnumber those who are against you if you've put your life and trust in His care.

He is the same God today as He was during Elisha's time and as He will be in the days to come. The Word is very clear: "For I am the LORD, I do not change" (Malachi 3:6). There are many churches today that dismiss "unanswered" prayers with the lie that God is not who He used to be. My God is not the Great I Was. His Word doesn't say, "I was bigger," "I was faithful," "I was all powerful," "I was all present." He is Ehyeh-Asher-Ehyeh, the Great I Am. "And God said to Moses, 'I AM WHO I AM'" (Exodus 3:14). His Word reveals Him as the Great I Am! "I Am bigger," "I Am faithful," "I Am with you always," He is not the

God who used to heal, He is Jehovah Rapha, the God who heals: "For I am the LORD who heals you" (Exodus 15:26). As we look upon our circumstances, we must keep our perspective or view in line with His Truth. His ways are higher and His timing is perfect. Regardless of what we see, hear, or feel, He *is* faithful and He *is* present.

Just as our view can be narrowed as we look upon our lives, it can also be narrowed as we focus upon God. How easily we can get stuck on one little drop of what God did and fail to see what He is doing or what He longs to do. He's not a "do things the same way twice" kind of God.

During a friend's quest for healing, she encountered many ministries that claimed they'd found *the* way to get healed. They offered classes, seminars, and group counseling sessions with a typed prayer and some form of a guaranteed, foolproof, seven-step solution for healing. Some do receive healing through such venues, but many who wholeheartedly pray that prayer and perform those seven steps walk away still battling sickness with the added burden of failure in their hearts. They believe they must have done something wrong because it didn't work for them. Many spend years going through those same seven steps repeatedly, hoping to get it right the next time. When that fails, they seek the next ministry that guarantees it knows how to shake a healing out of God's hands.

Many incredible ministries offer awesome testimony of God's divine healing, and we wholeheartedly rejoice in these miracles. We can glean foundational truths from what other believers have experienced. Our testimonies are be powerful, but God isn't a God of formulas, and He certainly doesn't withhold healing from His children simply because they haven't begged hard enough or jumped through the right hoops.

There is promise of healing in the Word, but it's not by our works that healing comes. I have failed to find *the* formula for healing in the Bible. Jesus healed many. In one story, He spit in the dirt and covered a man's face with mud. In another account, He told a proud nobleman to bathe in a dirty river, and a woman was healed simply by grasping His robe. One healing came by way of a boss asking Jesus to heal his servant. One child needed more than a healing, and a resurrection took place after one of God's prophets literally lay on top of the child's lifeless body.

In some cases, healing came by one word from His lips, and in others, by a touch of His hand. There's an account of people lining a road with sick friends and family members in hopes they would be healed simply by a man's shadow passing by them. He has not developed formulas to meet our needs—He *is* the formula. He encounters us individually and in each circumstance differently. Sadly, many have abandoned their search for Him to seek a formula.

As we wrestle with the whys, the why so longs, and the why some but not others, let us remind ourselves of the bigger picture.

> Now as Jesus passed by, He saw a man who was blind from birth. And His disciples asked Him, saying, "Rabbi, who sinned, this man or his parents, that he was born blind?" Jesus answered, "Neither this man nor his parents sinned, but that the works of God should be revealed in him." (John 9:1–3)

I wonder how many times his mother cried out for her child to be healed. In those days, a blind man's future was sure to include begging, and it is evident that a family who bore a sick child was believed to be a family living in sin, even in the eyes of those who walked with Jesus. This hardship hadn't been allowed in that man's life because of sin or lack of faith, or because he didn't read his Bible yesterday, or because his family hadn't prayed hard enough; it was because God had a plan to use his blindness for something great.

Can you imagine how incredible it would have been to be that man on the day his eyes were opened? How precious sight was to him; more precious than it is to any who don't know what it is like to not see. How his family's eyes must have welled up with tears when Jesus Himself cleared the family name in front of all who had cast judgment upon them. What other families found peace when it was announced publicly that not all children born with abnormalities are born into punishment?

Jesus answered the whys: "It's not because I don't love him, not because I haven't heard him, not because I'm not big enough, not because he's not one of the special ones. It's not because I don't care, not because I can't, not because I won't! It's because I have a divine timing for him and his life. I have healed him right here and now so you, My disciples, will encounter Me, My power, and My love. It's because his generation will get a taste of Me and see I am good. It's because I chose to put this man's story in My Book that will be read by billions over thousands of years. His story will infuse future generations with the courage to face the giants in their promised lands. Many will read his account and find hope, freedom, life, strength, and Me."

What higher perspective does God have on your life and circumstances? What are you actually asking God for when you ask Him to do it now? Could there be a person, a family, a nation, or a generation that will be affected by His diving timing in your life?

Where does the mind-set come from, that convinces us we fail in some biblical application because life is hard? Life on Earth is not about man climbing as high up the ladder as his legs and lifetime will carry him, acquiring as much wealth as he can before he dies. Nor is it about living lives of luxury, possessing the Midas touch where everything immediately turns to gold and everywhere we go flowers bloom and music plays. That sounds silly, but in reality, what do we expect from God while we're here? If we aren't expecting a happy-go-lucky life, we won't feel disappointed and betrayed by Him when things go wrong.

If I take a real look at my heart's expectations, I see a struggle of what I feel I'm entitled to as a Christian and the reality of living in a fallen world in which God promises me I'll face trials. There are those who teach if believers are experiencing hardships, they are out of God's will in some area of their lives. The Word is very clear that if we're living in sin, we give the enemy permission to access our lives, and there are consequences to disobeying His Word, but this doesn't mean all the difficulties we face are a result of unresolved sin in our lives.

It was said that Alexander the Great had an army of soldiers who were so completely surrendered to him and his cause they willingly marched off a cliff at his command. Whether or not this actually happened, there are many today who willingly sacrifice their lives for their countries, causes, or religious beliefs. Some have even strapped bombs to themselves believing that in doing so they were fulfilling their purpose on Earth. For these, their lives are not for their comfort; they exist solely to carry out the will of the king, country, or god they serve. They truly have surrendered their will to someone else's.

I have voiced my own surrender to my King's will: "Use me, God, to further Your Kingdom." But I have found that many times my surrender came with my will still intact. "Pick me, God, but can You pick me for the fun assignments, not the messy ones?" Messy assignments can be as simple as showing love to that co-worker who drives everyone crazy at the office or befriending the nerd at school or giving someone our time in the midst of our busyness. He is the God who is so enamored by the one missing sheep, that He will leave the other ninety-nine to seek that one. In His eyes, the assignment given to the war general leading a nation into battle to rescue an entire country, is no greater an assignment, than sending a teen into the lunchroom, to sit by a lonely new kid. Our paradigm shift must come with realization that our lives are not about us at all; we live for Him, His will, His purposes, and His Kingdom coming to Earth as it is in Heaven.

Has our God ever asked something of you that required your taking a giant leap out of your comfort zone? In such moments, we're swallowed up in self-focus and the impact one leap of obedience will have on us. Maybe your leap will set a generation free. Though we might at times find a difference in our levels of surrender to our King's will in comparison with that of Alexander's soldiers, we'll definitely find a difference in the leadership of our King versus that of Alexander the Great. Our King has placed a longing in our hearts to fulfill the calls He asks us to carry out. He offers to transform our hearts to match the sacrifices He requires of us. He promises to strengthen us to do the job, fight the battle, or travel the road. Our King loves us and delights in giving us the desires of our hearts.

God wants to have a relationship with as many people as will choose Him and to use those who have chosen Him to reach those who have yet to do so. That should be our cause. What if His allowing a wilderness experience in your life brings a nation to repentance? I seek to have my view shifted; my life here is not for my comfort but for His will to be fulfilled through me.

What do you want to see when you get to the end of your days and look back on them? We all have memories that are as real and fresh as the minute we first lived them. I have several, and one in particular replays as I contemplate my answer to this question. I'm sitting at a round table in the room we call the upper room. The church staff meeting is always on a Thursday. I'm barely twenty, and one of our executive pastors is up at the podium glancing at his notes for the day's discussions. I'm digging a pen out of my purse when he stops mid–bullet point and quotes 2 Timothy 4:7: "I have fought the good fight, I have finished the race, I have kept the faith." Tears are dripping from many familiar faces, and I realize Ann has just left us and is in this very moment face-to-face with Jesus.

There were no better or truer words to be said of my mentor. Ann was an amazing woman of God, a mother to a dear friend, a wife of a big-hearted pastor, an incredible leader in our church. She taught me how to fight for freedom while equipping me to teach others to do the same. She was passionate about God. I pray and seek to live my life as she did, wholeheartedly running the race set before me by my Maker.

When my last day comes, I want to look back and know, that I, through His grace and strength, gave everything I had within me to give to everyone who was placed around me to receive it. I don't know why God didn't answer our prayers to heal her here on Earth, or why He let her to leave us when she did. I do know she's completely healed and living in Heaven with Him. He is the God who healed her.

We have to place our trust in Him, not in what He will do. There's no better example for us than Daniel 3. Shadrach, Meshach, and Abed-Nego were given the death penalty for refusing to worship King Nebuchadnezzar's handmade gods. He questioned them before throwing them into the firey furnace, "Who is the god who will deliver you from my hands?" They replied,

> O Nebuchadnezzar, we have no need to answer you in this matter. If that is the case, our God whom we serve is able to deliver us from the burning fiery furnace, and He will deliver us from your hand, O king. But if not, let it be known to you, O king, that we do not serve your gods, nor will we worship the gold image which you have set up. (Daniel 3:15–18)

They let him know their God was able to deliver them, but if He chose not to, they were going to obey and serve Him even unto death. They placed all their trust in Him, not in what He would do.

How do we shift our focus? It's not always as simple as cleaning that mirror; at times, we'll need divine help in the shifting process.

Have you ever been trapped in a view? At times, no matter how hard I tried to redirect my thoughts, they continued to be consumed by one conversation I'd had or one action I'd taken. Regret is often fueled by a view we mentally replay.

As a high school and college athlete, I had my share of injuries. One time, I pulled a calf muscle, and it was painful. Every step hurt, and no matter what I was thinking about, that pain took over my thoughts instantly. I was convinced my injury would get better on its own, but each day, my limp got worse until I could barely stand.

I finally went to the doctor and learned my injury wouldn't heal without crutches and lots of sitting. I've never been good at sitting for long, and until the injury healed, it consumed my thoughts.

Emotional injuries are no different. They impact more than just the one troubled relationship or failed venture. Such wounds often flow out of our hearts and overrun our countenances, eating habits, energy levels, ability to sleep, and our relationships. We try to think about something else until someone unknowingly says one word that pushes that wound causing pain that once again consumes our minds. Just as is the case with physical injuries, until the emotional hurt stops, our minds are invaded.

So how do we stop the pain? Different injuries require different treatments. Some views will not be shifted until our hearts are healed. This too is a commonly misunderstood act of God's grace. He doesn't want us to stay wounded; open wounds rob so much from us and our loved ones, and they are always susceptible to infection if untreated. At times, He will leave us stuck with a view to make us face things we'd rather forget.

How do we heal? Sometimes, simply baring our all before Him in our prayer closet is enough, and this is by far the only place to start the journey. He is our Healer; He will let us know what steps we should take. My favorite verse regarding His direction is Psalm

32:8: "I will instruct you and teach you in the way you should go; I will guide you with My eye."

He loves to be face-to-face with us. My parents could speak volumes with their eyes. One look of warning directed us to stop what we were doing immediately or face the consequences. There was the "Come here now" look, the "That's my girl" look, the "Keep it up" look, and the "We'll see" look. We can know Him so well that one look in His eyes can speak volumes to us. He will direct us in our healing process.

The foundational steps to healing always include forgiving. My four-year-old and I were discussing how hard it is to forgive those who have wronged us. She's so great at putting her feelings into words. She simply said what my heart had many times felt: "I don't want to forgive, Mommy. And it's not easy to do." A lot of beliefs change between ages four and thirty, but this isn't one of them. He has taught me forgiveness is not contingent on a feeling. We can't wait until we feel like forgiving because that may never happen. Those who have hurt us may not deserve our forgiveness, but if we forgave only those who deserved it, none of us would be able to walk with God. The Bible is very clear: to be forgiven, we must forgive. He is not disappointed when we struggle to forgive; He waits for us to ask for the strength to do it, and He always gives it to those who ask.

He has also taught me that forgiveness is a process. I'd like the microwave version, but it doesn't exist. I used to get beat up by the enemy when after praying heartfelt prayers of forgiveness I'd be hurt again by the same person and all the wrongs I'd just forgiven came back to the forefront of my mind and reignited my emotions. Unforgiveness and hurt are like magnets; one attracts the other. Until the hurt is healed, unforgiveness will linger. Without the forgiveness part, the healing part doesn't happen.

As I struggled through the healing process of what felt like an impossible feat, God gave me a picture to carry me through. Every time I felt the hurt from the one I thought was my friend,

I would instantly forgive and repeatedly ask God for healing. Just when the enemy would whisper or shout into my ear that I was insincere or crippled for life, I would see the picture God gave me of my wound represented as a tree. With every cry of forgiveness and prayer for healing, I saw myself taking an axe to the tree's massive trunk. I refused to quit knowing that there would be an instance when I would forgive, the tree would fall, and my healing would be complete.

I've faced many such "trees" of hurt throughout my journey, some with little trunks felled by one swing of the axe, and several that took more swings than I could count, but my God healed me. I look back over the stumps and remember nothing is impossible with Him.

Two things that really help in this time of waiting for the hurt to heal are asking for His eyes for the people who have wronged us and praying sincere blessings over them. It's amazing how your heart can change toward even the most vicious person when you ask God to show you what He sees when He looks at him or her. And it's compounded when you begin to pray for them to have the very things your heart desires for yourself.

For You will light my lamp; The LORD my God will enlighten my darkness. (Psalm 18:28)

It's amazing how your view can be completely changed simply by turning on the light. Have you ever felt so in the dark about a situation that you didn't have a clue what was in front of you? Darkness seems to carry a connotation of depression or oppression, but sometimes, darkness is simply being unable to see where you are and what's coming.

Even familiar things look different in the dark. I still laugh remembering a movie scene where the main character finally crawls into his bed after a long day and rolls over to find that perfect cozy spot. Seconds later he sits straight up, almost paralyzed with fear. He quietly grabs a magazine from his bedside, rolls it tight, and begins inching his way across the room with a little ray of moonlight illuminating the floor. He stiffens as he makes it over to the wall. It takes him a moment to gather up the courage but once he does, he takes his magazine and lets loose, beating an enormous spider to death. The poor empty hook on the wall takes quite a beating before he realizes there was never a gigantic spider looming in his bedroom.

Sometimes, we just need God to turn on the lights for us. Psalm 18 promises He will give us light in dark places, but like all God's promises, we have to claim it. An unopened gift will not open itself. It will sit as do so many other amazing, powerful, unopened gifts given to us by our Creator. We have to ask Him for whatever we need. Why should we ask if He knows all things? The answer to that question could make up a whole book in and of itself.

> Ask, and it will be given to you; seek, and you will find; knock, and it will be opened to you. For everyone who asks receives, and he who seeks finds, and to him who knocks it will be opened. (Matthew 7:7–9)

> If you ask anything in My name, I will do it. (John 14:14)

> If you abide in Me, and My words abide in you, you will ask what you desire, and it shall be done for you. (John 15:7–8)

If we have no other answer, this one should be enough: we should ask Him for what we need because He tells us to. We all used to cringe when our parents answered our "Why?" with "Because I said so!" We can find more incredible truths about Him and His nature in an in-depth answer to this question, but if we trust Him, we can take Him at His Word and ask Him because that's what He tells us to do.

We start by asking Him to change our view. He might answer, "Not until you let me heal the hurt." He might shine His light or shift our view taking us past a spot on the surface to seeing the bigger picture through the window. God may simply refresh us and give us the strength to stay the course, and if it takes a wait, we can't give up, for the future of an entire nation might be hinging on our obedience.

Chapter Four

The Dream

> *The journey of life, then, is meant to be a dream quest; finding what your Maker has dreamed for you brings life's ultimate satisfaction and should be life's ultimate pursuit. If you don't discover God's dreams, you'll either waste your life running in wrong races and crossing wrong finish lines or, like many people, have no finish line at all.*[1]
> —Dutch Sheets

During one of the toughest seasons of my life, a dear friend of mine encouraged me to read Bruce Wilkinson's book *The Dream Giver*.[2] I cried the whole way through it. It's a story of a man who leaves his familiar, comfortable life to pursue his God-given dream and calling.

He begins by hearing that still, small voice of God waking him in the middle of the night, stirring his heart to believe he is called to do something huge. The urging becomes so heavy that he realizes he could live the rest of his life in mediocrity or take the biggest risk of his life and step out of his home into an unknown journey to an unknown land. All his friends and family try everything they can to dissuade him from his ridiculous endeavor, yet he decides to leave it all behind and blindly trust the Dream Giver rather than the other voices around him.

He faces many hardships along the way, but the one that gripped me the most was when the Dream Giver asked him to lay his dream down and walk away. If you've read his journey up to this point you are aware that everything he now lived for and everything he left behind was all for the fulfillment of this dream. The One who had asked him to forsake all, the One who had promised to fulfill his dream, was the One asking him to give it up. If you have ever walked this journey, you know this experience leaves you having to remind yourself to breathe.

Not to spoil the story for you (and I encourage you to read it), I have to tell you that he does receive his dream back from the Dream Giver, but what is left untold is how long he waited and what he experienced during his wait. I found myself longing for those details as I stood in the moment of just laying my own God-given dream on the altar.

Most of us are familiar with Abraham's experience. God called him to leave everything behind to journey to an unknown place. And in Genesis 15, God told him in a vision that his descendants would be as uncountable as the stars. Miraculously, God created life through him and his wife when they were well past their childbearing years.

But in Genesis 22, his Dream Giver asked him to sacrifice his son along with all the promises he had been given of becoming a great nation. We are never told what went through Abraham's mind; we read only that he got up the next morning and set out to kill his son and thus his dream.

I cannot begin to compare any experience I've endured with being asked to physically take my child's life. I can't even go there much less find words to share with you on this subject, but God does ask us to surrender everything and everyone into His hands and care. Once again, we are confronted with God operating in ways we cannot comprehend. Abraham obeyed, and God intervened at the last minute; He provided a ram for the sacrifice, sparing Isaac's life and restoring Abraham's dream.

But there is something that happens when we willingly choose to lay our dreams down at God's feet. These God-given dreams are of such magnitude that they could easily destroy us by becoming the most important thing in our lives, something we might choose to place even above God Himself. It is His loving grace that requires us to make such painful sacrifices at times. He will test our hearts to ensure our dreams will not destroy us or those we are intended to reach before allowing us to pick them back up again.

What's your dream? It could be a promise laid out for you in the Bible, one of healing, deliverance, restoration, provision, direction, joy, or peace. Do you feel like Jeremiah being consumed with the Words of God like "fire shut up in [your] bones" that you feel you might explode if you don't get to preach (Jeremiah 7:9)? Maybe there's a book being birthed in you. Is there a canvas awaiting your paintbrush, a song you long to share, a people you want to reach? Maybe you were born to start an amazing new business. Do you yearn to find a cure the world is seeking? If you don't have an answer, ask God what He has woven into your being to fulfill, and He will reveal it to you.

The wait is always different. We wait like Habakkuk for God to fix our brokenness; we wait like one who has the promise of healing yet faces the symptoms and miseries of sickness. We wait like Joseph, the young boy who had God-given dreams of ruling and reigning, sitting in a prison cell for crimes he never committed and wondering if he had really heard God to begin with (Genesis 40). We wait like David, who after being anointed king, went to sit alone with his father's sheep and fight off lions and bears. We wait like one who has abandoned the comfort of home in the face of ridicule to reach our promised land and walk out our God-given dream only to have been asked to lay it down, not knowing if or when we'll get to carry it again.

One of the biggest questions I asked during this season of waiting for ministry doors to once again be opened was, "What does 'faithful' look like in the midst of the wait?" It starts by simply being faithful with what you've already been given. You have been given a promise; what are you doing with that promise right now? Are you praying over it? Are you educating yourself in it? Are you making declarations into the spiritual realm regarding it?

> Well done, good and faithful servant; you were faithful over a few things, I will make you ruler over many things. (Matthew 25:21)

The testing of our hearts and readiness for the fulfillment of our dream starts the moment the dream is first given to us. If we can't be faithful with the promise of the dream, we most certainly can't be faithful with the walking out of the dream.

Another book recommended to me during this same time by the same friend was Andy Stanley's *Visioneering*.[3] If your wait is for the fulfillment of your divine calling, this book is a must read. He discusses the importance of preparing for your dream the moment it's realized: "Plan as if you knew someone was going to come along and give you an opportunity to pursue your vision" and "Develop a strategy. Dream on paper." You have a responsibility right now to ready yourself for your dream.

This book started out as one of my dreams, but it took me years to write it. Dreams are often birthed as seed. Seeds aren't much to look at; they're small, ugly, and dry, yet seeds are carriers of life. They have the potential to become much more in time. In fact, they are so insignificant, many are lost before ever reaching their potential. It's hard to believe that just one of those annoying apple seeds in the center of your afternoon snack has the potential to produce millions of new apples. How many apple seeds are thrown away?

God breathes dreams inside His people as seed. The moment we hear His promise or see His vision, we become carriers of the life of our God-given seed. What we do with our seed will play a huge role in what will become of it.

Many say God's plans will happen in our lives regardless of how we choose to live. If this were true, everyone would choose to become a Christian; God's Word clearly states it is His will that all people be saved (2 Peter 3:9; 1 Timothy 2:4). He gave us freedom to choose Him and His Word as truth or reject them as false. The Bible is filled with choices He has given us that will impact our lives on Earth. When we receive His seed, whether the seed of His written Word or seed He speaks to us, we're entrusted with the outcome of those seeds in our lives. The parable of the talents in Matthew 25 and the parable of the sower in Matthew 13 demonstrate our responsibility to take what's given to us and protect, prepare for, and multiply it.

My girls and I love to plant things and watch them grow. But before we get to taste incredible fruit or enjoy gorgeous flowers, we have to bury our seeds in dirt. Around here it is common to add some unsavory elements to our gardens to enrich the soil and bring about a better crop. Isn't it exciting to hear that God has called us to great things? The moment we find out what He created us to do—our purpose, our calling—is exhilarating. Our hearts quicken at the thought that we could be used for something great! Receiving the seeds of our dreams is amazing, but the steps we must take to see them fulfilled are anything but.

> Most assuredly, I say to you, unless a grain of wheat falls into the ground and dies, it remains alone; but if it dies, it produces much grain. (John 12:24)

God-given dreams can be so big they are hard to believe. That is probably what Abraham and Sarah thought when God breathed their dream.

> As for Me, behold, My covenant is with you, and you shall be a father of many nations. No longer shall your name be called Abram, but your name shall be Abraham; for I have made you a father of many nations. I will make you exceedingly fruitful; and I will make nations of you, and kings shall come from you. (Genesis 17:4–6)

People lived longer in those days and had much bigger families, but for Abraham and Sarah, the reality of having a large family was naturally impossible. Sarah was barren, and these two lovebirds were well past their childbearing years. We often hear that verse about God's ways being bigger and higher than ours in the context of not understanding Him, but in these dream-giving moments, God's plans for us far exceed our imaginations. This dream was so far-fetched that Sarah actually laughed in her heart when she heard the promise. Does God's dream for you seem beyond belief? Do you struggle to let yourself hope for something big? I love God's response to Sarah's laughter.

> And the Lord said to Abraham, "Why did Sarah laugh, saying, 'Shall I surely bear a child, since I am old?' Is anything too hard for the Lord? At the appointed time I will return to you, according to the time of life, and Sarah shall have a son." (Genesis 18:13–14)

God wants us to honor Him by believing He can do the impossible in us, for us, and through us. He is glorified when the impossible, made possible, points to Him alone.

Once we are given our dreams, we must plant them deep in prayer and faith to protect them. What does the soil look like? The first step in seed care is simply this: write it down! I love this verse in Habakkuk 2:2 "Write the vision and make it plain on tablets, that he may run who reads it." Something about putting your dream on paper breathes life into it. If nothing else explains this, it takes faith to believe in it enough to put in on paper. Writing it births the strength to run towards it. I keep my God-given dreams in a prayer journal. I write them, I surrender them to God, and ask Him to have His way on Earth as it is in Heaven with the dream or promise I receive.

While our seed lies buried in dirt and fertilizer, God begins preparing us for the fruitful season that will follow in time. This preparation period is very often like stepping into Mr. Miyagi's *dojo* in the movie *The Karate Kid*. Young Daniel LaRusso is in desperate need to learn self-defense, and Mr. Miyagi agrees to train him as long as he will do these three things: show up, work hard, and ask no questions. The eager student quickly agrees, and his training begins.

Day after day, Daniel-Son shows up, but class doesn't take place in a gym or dojo. The karate lessons are taught in Mr. Miyagi's own yard. For days, he washes and waxes a front yard full of classic cars. Next, he spends more days sanding floors, staining both sides of a somewhat never-ending fence, and painting his sensei's house.

It seems to him bad enough that Mr. Miyagi hasn't held up his end of the bargain to train him in karate, but he has also taken advantage of him. To top it all off, while Daniel-Son sweats it out, Mr. Miyagi goes fishing. Daniel finally reaches the breaking point and begins to ask questions; he finds his wise sensei has been teaching him karate all along. The motions of waxing, sanding, and painting have given his body the basic karate skills he will need to become a great fighter.

King David's *dojo* was a lonely field full of sheep. In 1 Samuel 16, we read of a young shepherd being chosen and even anointed king of Israel. That was the moment he discovered his dream, but the day after he was anointed as king, he went back to tending his father's sheep. No one around him could see his royal crown. God trained him while his seed germinated in the dark soil. It was in a field of sheep that David learned how to fight. He became skilled with a slingshot, the very weapon that would soon be used to set an entire nation free.

But he didn't know defeating Goliath was in his future; he was simply being faithful with where God had placed him. His faithfulness as a shepherd prepared him to be a great king. While the shepherd boy was fighting off lions and bears with his bare hands to protect his father's sheep, his Sensei was developing boldness deep inside him. This boldness would soon be needed to face off with a giant that made an entire army tremble in fear.

The loneliness of that field pushed him to draw near to God. His season of friendlessness enabled him to know God as his best friend. This intimate relationship with God was what made his reign as commander of the Israelite army so successful. And his skilled harp playing was later used to grant him much-needed favor with King Saul. His dojo went from the field to the cave of Adullam. David had to flee for his life when the king became jealous. King Saul was out to destroy David's dream before it came to be.

David chose to be patient and humble. If he chose pride and refused the dojo of the pasture, he wouldn't have slain the giant that threatened his future kingdom. He wouldn't have been able to trust in his God in all the battles that awaited him. The cave of Adullam was a choice he made to protect his dream.

I've seen many dreams snuffed out because the dreamer felt he was entitled to the fruit of the dream before it had been produced. If David had chosen to dishonor his dishonorable authority, if he in self-defense had decided to kill King Saul instead of fleeing to the cave, he would have missed out on God's blessings and training.

David departed from there and escaped to the cave of Adullam. And when his brothers and all his father's house heard it, they went down there to him. And everyone who was in distress, and everyone who was in debt, and everyone who was bitter in soul, gathered to him. And he became commander over them. And there were with him about four hundred men. (1 Samuel 22:1–2)

Another one of my favorite dojo experiences in the Bible is that of Nehemiah's captivity. I absolutely love Nehemiah; I look forward to meeting him when I get Home. He had been taken captive in war and made to serve the enemy king. He must have had ample opportunity to carry out revenge as he was the king's cupbearer. The men and women God uses to do great things will have to choose forgiveness before they reach the fulfillment of their God-given dreams. As we set out to protect our seed, we must guard against bitterness, which will choke the life out of our dreams.

Nehemiah had a dream to see his nation restored. He longed to see the city walls that had been destroyed in war rebuilt, but he also yearned to see his people following God again. When he learned the condition of his war-torn homeland, he grieved, fasted, prayed, and wept. He understood that his captivity positioned him in a place of favor with the enemy king. He saw the king almost daily when he brought him his wine, but in his brokenness he couldn't put on a good face. His dream caused him to grieve for others.

God calls some to carry the weight of lost loved ones or even lost nations in their hearts. I cry many tears for people and my tears are not understood by most. I've found that protecting my seed requires me to be okay with crying misunderstood tears. I was praying in my bedroom my senior year in high school when my surrender of tears took place. I have forgotten what I started out praying about that day, but God somehow directed our conversation to tears.

I didn't cry at that time of my life, and as I told God, "I don't cry," He whispered, "I do!" He offered me an invitation to be one who would cry with Him; would I allow His brokenness for the broken to be felt and cried for, in my own heart? Anytime we surrender something to God, He gives us more than what we give away. My heart grieves for people deeply, but my heart also loves and celebrates deeply. I didn't know this was part of the deal when I said yes to the tears. God is so good.

Some ask, why tears? The enemy has tried to stop my tears many times. I've had to search Scripture to remain confident in them. I found those who were called to do spiritual warfare over nations were given a burden for the people from God. This burden was the fuel that enabled them to liberate those in captivity. Jesus healed people out of compassion for them (Matthew 14:14). It's easy to forget there are different assignments in God's Kingdom; each assignment looks different. We aren't all called to cry, not all fight on the front lines.

Nehemiah wept over his nation, and his grief overtook his countenance for days. The king sensed his grief and asked him, "Why is your face sad, since you are not sick? This is nothing but sorrow of heart" (Nehemiah 2:2). Can you imagine the king caring enough about his servant to ask him what was wrong? Nehemiah was his servant, but he was also his enemy, a prisoner of war.

God's dojo for Nehemiah was captivity. It was there that he learned patience, self-control and how to forgive his enemies. He had to put others first. He had to serve the king whose people burned his land and had taken him from his home. In captivity, God granted him favor with his enemy. In response to the king's question about his sad face, Nehemiah boldly poured his brokenness of heart out before the king. He was willing to risk his life for those he carried in his heart. His tears gave him boldness to ask King Artaxerxes for permission to go back and rebuild his war-torn homeland, for letters of safe passage, and for the materials he needed for rebuilding the city walls. "And the king granted them to me according to the good hand of my God upon me" (Nehemiah 2:8b).

We shouldn't "despise the day of small beginnings" (Zechariah 4:10). God uses seemingly small things to train us for bigger ones. If we are seeking Him above our dreams and taking each next step of obedience, we can rest in His grace and peace as we wait.

God is a good steward of our gifts, passions, and time. He will use our circumstances to prepare us for what He alone sees ahead on our journeys. He won't send us into battles He hasn't first prepared us to win. But we have to trust Him regardless of what our dojo experiences look and feel like.

How do we know if our dreams are simply our grand desires or if they come from God? The Bible will always confirm His plans. Search the Word; what does it say about your dream? Ask God for confirmation, and seek wise counsel. Our biggest tool during this time of seed protecting, dojo journeying, and dream waiting is in Matthew 6:33: "But seek ye first the kingdom of God, and his righteousness; and all these things shall be added unto you." If we are faithful to keep Him first, seek Him, listen, and quickly do whatever He asks of us, He will open the doors for our dreams to come true.

We all have a purpose here, a personal, God-given dream. To see our dreams become reality, we must position ourselves to receive His life-bearing seeds. We must protect them at all costs, bury them in the soil of God's leading, consistently water them with our faith and prayers, and be faithful to God in the dojos He provides us.

Chapter Five

The Rod

*Many men owe the grandeur of their
lives to tremendous difficulties.*[1]
—Charles H. Spurgeon

Several years ago, I got to go on the trip of a lifetime to Israel. It was amazing to walk into the scenes of my favorite Bible stories. Daily life is quite different there. One day, we were traveling a very dangerous and bumpy road. I was prone to carsickness, and when I could no longer endure the back of the bus, I made my way to the front and sat on the step so I could look out the windshield. It was in that moment that I learned one of the daily life differences between their culture and ours.

Anton, our guide, was a precious man who never stopped to take a breath throughout our two-week trip. He always stood at the front of the bus and spoke a wealth of information through the little bus microphone and as I sat down to regain my color, I found myself nose high to his armpits. There are things I might forget here and there, but my daily deodorant application is not one of them and in Israel the people's getting-ready routine doesn't include deodorant. I realized I wouldn't be regaining my color any time soon.

> Now Amalek came and fought with Israel in Rephidim. And Moses said to Joshua, "Choose us some men and go out, fight with Amalek. Tomorrow I will stand on the top of the hill with the rod of God in my hand." So Joshua did as Moses said to him, and fought with Amalek. And Moses, Aaron, and Hur went up to the top of the hill. And so it was, when Moses held up his hand, that Israel prevailed; and when he let down his hand, Amalek prevailed. But Moses' hands became heavy; so they took a stone and put it under him, and he sat on it. And Aaron and Hur supported his hands, one on one side, and the other on the other side; and his hands were steady until the going down of the sun. So Joshua defeated Amalek and his people with the edge of the sword. (Exodus 17:8–13)

It's amazing to read through the Old Testament battles, they were all so different. One was won by a teenager slinging a rock while another was won by an army marching in circles. Many of us have heard Bible stories for so long that they seem to be fairy tales, stories in a good book, not real-life experiences. Picture our soldiers in Iraq or Afghanistan hearing their commander say, "No weapons today, guys. We'll beat these terrorists by walking around in circles."

Some battles were won by lining the front line not with archers but musicians. Can you picture the look on their enemies' faces when the front line pulled out harps instead of arrows? They must certainly have thought they had that one in the bag, but they didn't.

One battle was won by soldiers digging ditches in an empty field. During the night God miraculously filled them with water. The next morning, the enemy, believed the field was covered in pools of blood and confidently charged the Israelites' camp to take the spoil. They arrived to find the Israelite army thriving and ready to destroy them (2 Kings 3:16–27).

In another war, victory came when each soldier broke a piece of pottery and yelled a cheer simultaneously at the top of their lungs. I love the time God caused a deep sleep to fall upon the entire army of the enemy. One of my favorites is when God took the wheels off the Egyptians chariots. Those guys were just out of luck; there's nothing you can do when God starts flicking the wheels off your chariot.

There are many more unique war stories in the Old Testament. He chose to use a completely different strategy with each battle because He wants us to come to Him every day. He's not a boring God. He's always doing something in a new way; He makes life exciting. The Creator must love us; He could have given us the need to eat without including our taste buds, or He could have given us the ability to reproduce without the enjoyment aspect. I think the world has forgotten that God created sex, and they accuse Him of not wanting them to have any fun. The Word says He created the beautiful scenery for us to enjoy. He made life on Earth pleasurable, and He did so with us in mind.

In this battle in Exodus 17, God gave Moses the winning strategy: when the army took the field, Moses was to climb up the hill; when they wielded their swords, Moses was to lift his rod. No matter how hard those soldiers swung their swords or how quick they were on their feet, they were winning only when Moses held up that rod. When his arms tired and he let them down, they began to lose.

No matter how strong we are, if we aren't battling according to God's strategy, we're gonna lose. We can discipline our minds and bodies and build up our spiritual muscles, but if we don't seek Him each time we face a threat to our family, church or nation, we won't know how to pray or what weapon God has called us to wield.

Israel's future was impacted by Moses' obedience to seek God and do what He instructed him to do no matter how ridiculous it might have made him look. We live in a time where identifying leaders in any venue who are more concerned about how they look before God, than how they look before men, seems impossible. I find myself watching the news, longing for our leaders who have been given the privilege to lead in our government, billion dollar companies, and in the Church use their God-given talents to stand up and *lead*, making decisions that will impact people rather than a title, paycheck, or popularity vote.

Moses led his people with integrity; he carried the weight of the nation of Israel on his shoulders, and when he realized the burden was too heavy, he humbled himself and asked for help. The entire nation was dependent on his willingness to be vulnerable. He had to admit he couldn't do it alone; he was the leader, but he needed help. He also had to allow Aaron and Hur so close to him they would see and smell the areas of his life that weren't perfect. They had to be at nose level with his armpits. If he had chosen to protect himself in pride, he would have sent many to their deaths. How many present day leaders have chosen the latter causing many to fall away from the truth in order to protect their perfect, plastic reputations? How many times have we suffered under a weight we could no longer carry alone because we were too proud to let others know we were weak?

There will be times we are unable to carry the weight of someone else upon our shoulders with our own strength, and times we'll need to help others carry their God-given burdens. Neither of these positions is easy. In the first situation, we have to be vulnerable, and in the second, we have to stand nose -level in the stinky parts of peoples lives to help them make it through their burden bearing. Not every burden we carry contains the weight of an entire nation, but we can be sure that every battle we fight will impact others.

By what names do you call your Aaron and Hur? Mine have had different names throughout the seasons of my life, but one thing has remained constant—God has always provided them when the battle required their strength. He promises in His Word to never leave or forsake us.

> When you are in distress, and all these things come upon you in the latter days, when you turn to the LORD your God and obey His voice (for the LORD your God is a merciful God), He will not forsake you nor destroy you, nor forget the covenant of your fathers which He swore to them. (Deuteronomy 4:30–31)
>
> Be strong and of good courage, do not fear or be afraid of them; for the LORD you God, He is the One who goes with you. He will not leave you nor forsake you. (Deuteronomy 31:6)

As my seasons have changed, so have the people around me. I went through a time when my closest friends were called to walk in a different direction, and God spoke a word to me that I carry into every season change: "I will always provide for you who you need, when you need them. Some will stay a part of your life while others will simply pass through." If you find yourself weak and tired, in need of someone to hold your arms up, ask Him. He will show you whom you can trust, and He will give you the courage to ask for their help and the strength to rest your arms in theirs.

Sometimes, our Aarons and Hurs do more than just hold up our arms. In one of the theology courses I took, we were told the amazing story of Felix Manz. He was born in Zurich, Switzerland in the late fifteenth century. He was passionate about God and believed He spoke to him and anyone else who wanted to hear Him. In his walk with the Lord, he came to believe that baptism was for those who willingly chose to repent of their sins and accept the new life given and promised through Jesus Christ.

This belief went against the church of Zurich, as it allowed only infant baptisms; anyone who took part in baptizing adults would be punished by drowning. Felix had been arrested many times for living out his beliefs, and this time would be no different. At twenty-something years old, Felix was sentenced to be drowned in the Limmat River.

Knowing it was his final hour on Earth, he chose his last words to be that of preaching the Word and worshipping His God. He wasn't pleading for God to give him more time; he wasn't fearful or angry; he didn't defend himself. He made every minute of his time in this place count. In the face of drowning, he was loving God and people, not focusing on himself. He must have thought that in his worship and preaching, some would come to know the truth.

While he was proclaiming the Word, a priest was doing all he could to convince Felix to change his mind. If he would have recanted, he might have lived beyond that day. God provided his Aaron and Hur. His mother and brother walked alongside him all the way to the river and remained on the shore until he took his last breath. The whole time, they spurred him on, shouting at him to stand strong and not give up. They told him how proud they were of him, conveying the message, "You can do this! We believe in you!"

The Israelites' victory in this battle came not from strength of sword or strategy of leadership; it came from faithfulness. If any person hadn't fulfilled his role, the people of Israel would have suffered. It took Moses' rod and vulnerability, the strength and availability of Aaron and Hur, and the swords of soldiers.

We have to remind ourselves every day that we live in a war zone that is not always seen, heard, or felt; it far surpasses our natural senses. Our enemy seeks not just to effect change in our land or further his cause; he's out to steal, kill, and destroy us; to separate us from God (John 10:10). Satan works to destroy individuals, families, generations, cities, states, and whole nations. He's an exceptionally skilled warrior; he's strategic, tenacious, motivated, and powerful. He seems to never tire and goes to any extreme to carry out his plans.

Our only hope, my lost loved ones' only hope, and America's only hope rest on our faithfulness in seeking God, waiting for His answer, and obeying His commands. In all the battles in the Bible, God never failed to bring victory to those who sought His counsel, waited until they heard His voice, and obeyed His commands.

In account after account, armies outnumbered beyond belief won, one man changed the destiny of his generation, and the faithfulness of one man transformed a nation. He is the same God today. If the Bible is true about our God, He can use one man to change the heritage of his family, one faithful politician to change the White House, and one redeemed sinner on her knees to effect change in her community.

The word *rod* in Exodus 17:9 is the Hebrew word *matteh*,[2] a "branch, tribe or rod." The Word often describes the people of God as branches attached to Him, the Vine. Moses held up before God the tribe and the people of Israel, and he didn't lay his burden down until his people had defeated their enemy.

Our world is full of nations, tribes, and people who are at war, but how many of those people carry their countries to God, refusing to rest until the battle is won? Many claim to be too busy and burdened to give anything to others, but are they busy with things God hasn't called them to handle? He has given us a command to love others and give from what He has given us. Maybe we have taken on more than we should have, or maybe we're carrying too much of life by ourselves. He said what He asks us to carry is easy and light.

Come to Me, all you who labor and are heavy laden, and I will give you rest. Take My yoke upon you and learn from Me, for I am gentle and lowly in heart, and you will find rest for your souls. For My yoke is easy and My burden is light. (Matthew 11:28–30)

This doesn't mean that life's trials are easy; the "rest" is given after we come. We have to go to Him and let Him take up our burdens. God will show us what to lay at His feet and what to do with what we are asked to carry. He gives us refreshing and divine strength, and He supplies others to help us when we need it. We have to enter into God's rest. We must be a people of faith who seek His face to direct our next move.

Are you called right now to wield a sword, hold a rod, or carry someone's burden? Have you heard Him speak to your heart regarding your present circumstances? If you struggle to hear His voice, read John 10. Romans 10:17 says, "So then faith comes by hearing, and hearing by the word of God."

If we lack faith in any area of life, we can look for bible verses about that topic and meditate on them until they become rooted in faith in our hearts. We forget the Word of God is alive! Reading it changes us, and we need its life and power. Our families, our neighbors, and our countries can't afford for us to remain powerless, unable to hear His voice, and without a strategy to win our battles.

Why a rod? The Hebrew and Greek words for *rod* have almost identical definitions. A rod was a wooden stick used as a support on rough terrain, a weapon to ward off attackers, a tool to separate grain from chaff, a unit of measurement, and a form of correction when a sheep or servant strayed. God and Moses had quite a history with a rod. Moses fled the rod of a scepter, leaving royalty behind him in Egypt to pick up the rod of a shepherd dwelling in the deserts of Midian.

When God met Moses at the burning bush, Moses asked God for proof to present to the Israelites that he was their God-given deliverer. He asked Moses what he had in his hand; it was his rod. The rod represented God's authority given to man to impart God's will on Earth, and it was something Moses already had. Moses carried the authority of the throne room of Heaven every day, yet it remained an untapped power because Moses didn't realize what he'd been given. He didn't know how to use it to its full potential until He met with God and heard Him say, "When you go back to Egypt, see that you do all those wonders before Pharaoh which I have put in your hand" (Exodus 4:21a).

When Moses and Aaron went before Pharaoh, their stick turned into a snake; when Pharaoh's sorcerers duplicated the act of power, Aaron's stick ate up the other sticks that had turned into snakes. The rod was used to turn the Nile into a river of blood, brought plagues on the Egyptians, divided the Red Sea, and caused water to flow out of a rock in the wilderness. But before any of these displays of God's power occurred, a man heard God speak and took action. He instructed them what to do with the authority He'd given them. Sometimes, the instruction was to lift the rod high, while other times, Moses was to take it and swing hard.

As the Israelites waited to walk into their Promised Land, they experienced incredible warfare. They fought many battles and didn't arrive in their new home without battle scars. I believe every God-given promised land comes filled with giants and our times of waiting can be war zones. The silver lining, of course, is that we walk into our war zones with our own God-given rods. What has He put in your hand that will bring about victory in your circumstances?

We must lean into Him to hear that still, small voice. Moses learned he carried a rod, but some of his lessons in how to use that rod turned out to be very pricey. The first time in the wilderness, he struck the rock as God had commanded to bring forth water. The second time, God instructed Moses to hold up the rod and speak to the rock. We remember that tragic moment when Moses went to the rock and struck it instead of speaking to it; his misuse of God's authority denied him the privilege of entering the Promised Land.

We've been given dominion and authority over Earth. We carry the power of the Creator of all things in our hands. God will hold us accountable for how we use or neglect to use what He has given us (Matthew 25).

Are you wandering in a wilderness? Many think of the desert the Israelites journeyed through as a place of punishment and misery, but it was never intended to be that; it was simply the land they had to travel through to reach the land of milk and honey. The wilderness was a hard but amazing place. Only in the wilderness does God deliver your dinner through the rain. It's in the wilderness that we understand God has control over the animals. It was there that He ordered the quail to wait outside tent doors to become dinner.

In the wilderness, we learn that no matter how hot, hard, empty, or dry it gets, He will always come through for us. The only guide we have in our wilderness is a pillar of cloud by day and a pillar of fire by night (Numbers 14:14). The Israelites grumbled and set their gaze upon what they lacked, refusing to see what God provided in His awe-filled, marvelous acts. Their ungrateful, self-centered hearts turned the wilderness into a place of punishment. But for Moses, it was the place where He saw God's face and heard His voice (Exodus 33:11).

Embrace your wilderness. That might sound impossible, but "nothing is impossible with God" (Luke 1:37). I have clung to others' words in the driest places of my own wilderness. Many times have I heard that the length of the wait and intensity of the training are indicators of the magnitude of the call upon our lives. The best wine is one that has aged the longest. The vessel used to hold the wine during its aging process has an incredible influence upon the wine. An oak barrel is deemed the best. As the wine rests inside, the character of the wood is imparted into the wine.

And as it ages, the barrel slowly allows oxygen in, resulting in a complexity of flavor and a softening of the harsh tannins produced by fermentation.

Who is holding you during your wait? Could it be that as He presses you into a wait, He is imparting His very character into yours and infusing you with life while softening the hard and bitter elements of your heart? He who promised the Promised Land is faithful.

> Let us hold fast the confession of
> our hope without wavering, for He
> who promised is faithful.
> —Hebrews 10:23

Chapter Six

The Season

> *I wonder if the snow loves the trees and fields, that it kisses them so gently? And then it covers them up snug, you know, with a white quilt; and perhaps it says, "Go to sleep darlings, till summer comes again."*[1]
> —Lewis Carroll

Some of my favorite childhood memories are those of waking up to fresh fallen snow glistening in our yard. The best part was getting bundled up to an almost unrecognizable state with my brother and sister and racing outside to make snow angels, catch flakes on our tongues, and make snowmen until our fingers froze.

We didn't have a garage, so we'd have to tromp through the snow-covered yard to our car on Sundays. I remember getting all dressed up in my little white tights and best dress and standing at the front door trying to figure out how I'd make it to the car. My father came up with a plan. He went a step at a time, making a way in the snow. I stayed behind him and put my little black Mary

Janes in his footprints. No matter how high that snow piled up, my tights stayed dry all the way to the car.

Years later, I was at the end of my first season as a youth minister. I was looking behind me, grieving, unknowing, uncertain of what lay ahead. I wasn't sure what was coming as God Himself moved me to resign. This was my moment where the Dream Giver asked me to lay down my dream and walk away. Ministry was all I wanted to do from sunup to sundown. Youth ministry was hard, but I loved it, and I never pictured myself in any other venue. I planned on living full-time ministry till the day God called me Home. Yet there I stood in the doorway, being told to leave with all my heart longing to stay and nothing in front of me but blankness. When I cried out to God, the only direction I received was to get behind Him and place my feet wherever I saw Him place His.

It was one of the hardest times of my life. I couldn't understand why God was making me leave after I had faithfully endured so much. My heart cried out to know why I was being punished. I had been through multiple battles while there and had given all I had to be faithful, to do the right thing no matter the cost. No other doors of ministry were opening to me, and I grieved. I grieved ministry for years. I hoped that season of being without my dream would be short. The verse, "Hope deferred makes the heart sick," was my new dwelling place (Proverbs 13:12). The hardest part was being in a place where no one understood my pain and the season leading up to that moment of walking away from my dream into the unknown was brutal.

I had been doing what I loved, living life with "my kids" for years, but soon after my seven-year mark, I began to struggle with passion; I no longer had any. God gave me a picture of myself strapping a refrigerator to my back like a backpack; it represented the weight of the ministry I carried. My fridge had come with big wheels on the bottom, enabling me to move forward with the fridge in tow. As my passion faded, so did the wheels, and I could no longer move.

The enemy was surrounding me like a vulture circling his next meal. His voice was so loud during that time that I found it difficult to hear anyone else's. I tried everything I could to reignite my passion, but nothing worked. The more I failed at it, the more I questioned the condition of my heart: *Am I in some major sin I don't know about?* I felt distant, disconnected from everyone around me, including my friends I had ministered with for years.

One day, I had a vision of a huge ship in the middle of the ocean with no land in sight. There was a rope connected to the ship, and way far away, tied to the other end, was a little buoy bobbing up and down all alone. The ship was the youth ministry, and the buoy was me. As I had been seeking His help in making sense of all this, He led me to study the process of transplanting trees.

God often uses natural processes and illustrations to help us connect our understanding to something He is doing in the spiritual realm. As I studied trees, I learned that a skilled gardener will wait until a tree is dormant before transplanting it. The next step is to sever all the roots by using a sharp tool and quick hands. A good-sized tree will lose about 75 percent of its roots. What intrigued me most was that a tree has a much better chance to survive if it's left in the ground with severed roots for one to two years before being moved.

Before moving a tree, a gardener will dig the new hole large enough to make room for new growth. After this process has been started, the tree will require intense watering. When the time finally comes to pull it out of the ground, it must be wrapped well in burlap to protect the stressed roots from the elements. Even after transplanting, the gardener will water the tree frequently; if it were to dry out, it would not survive the move. It will require extra watering for at least two years.

God revealed to me the season He had me in; He had severed my roots, which is why I felt so disconnected, but He hadn't yet taken me out of the ground. So I sat, planted but severed in the ground I had thrived in for over seven years.

When God transplants His people, He takes the best of care to do it right. Sometimes, He simply picks us up and replants us in the same yard. Other times, He plants us in a different area in the body of Christ. Have you ever been in a dormant season and been discouraged by the lack of fruit in your life? The enemy is quick to accuse us of failure, but we all have to endure dormant seasons before we can grow bigger in our springs. If we don't recognize the different seasons God carries us through, we'll be prime targets for discouragement.

I've had winters of waking up and running outside, frantically searching my tree for any signs of life. I expected to see leaves and green and blooms, but it was brown, brittle, and flowerless. If you find yourself in a fruitless state, ask the Gardner to reveal the season He has you in. Sometimes, we simply need to be fed or given more water; other times, we must wait through cold, dry days until spring arrives or until He moves us.

I began to understand why I felt so disconnected, but it didn't make it hurt less. I understood it was meant to make it easier on me and those around me when it came time to be pulled out of the ground. I also found myself in a place I'd never been before as I was on the verge of spiritual dehydration.

In my last months while on staff at the church and for the next two years in the secular work place, I thirsted. I would wake up in the morning and spend time with God, but by lunch I'd be parched. I spent my lunch hours reading, worshipping, praying, and crying, and that would give me just enough to make it through the afternoon. But the moment I got into my car, it started again.

I had women around me who had always been a refuge, but in that season, I was alone. Those I had leaned on and sought counsel from for years didn't understand my tears or my thirst. I questioned my heart: *What's wrong with me? What am I doing to allow this misery in my life? If my mentors don't understand why I'm in this condition, I must be in a wrong place.* I was right where God had led me, but because I was being transplanted, I needed lots of water. It is in this season that the tree must prepare to stand alone; for when it is replanted, it will not have the strong roots to hold it in place when the wind blows.

King Solomon, the wisest man ever to walk the Earth, understood this spiritual truth.

> To everything there is a season, A time for every purpose under heaven: A time to be born, And a time to die; A time to plant, And a time to pluck what is planted; A time to kill, And a time to heal; A time to break down, And a time to build up; A time to weep, And a time to laugh; A time to mourn, And a time to dance; A time to cast away stones, And a time to gather stones; A time to embrace, And a time to refrain from embracing; A time to gain, And a time to lose; A time to keep, And a time to throw away; A time to tear, And a time to sew; A time to keep silence, And a time to speak; A time to love, And a time to hate; A time of war, And a time of peace. (Ecclesiastes 3:1–8)

It's easy to blame our winter days on Satan, but we must keep in mind that God created the seasons. And since we know He is good all the time and takes care of us, there must be some good awaiting us in the winter.

> *The day is Yours, the night also is Yours; You have prepared the light and the sun. You have set all the borders of the earth; You have made summer and winter.* (Psalm 74:16–17)

The winter provides a time of rest and pushes us into that dormant place of stillness. When a tree stands bare, stripped of visible growth, people wonder if it will ever produce anything again. It is in winter we are forced to know our identities based upon our roots, and not our fruit. Our identities cannot be placed in the works we do or the ways others see the fruit of our labor; our identities must be found in who we are under the surface, where no one but God, Himself can see. We're forced to find our affirmation in Him, not in our successes, nor in completed to- do lists.

During these dormant days, we ask ourselves, *Is my worth based upon what I do or in who I am?* This season defines who we are and what we're made of; it's not a season during which we'll receive praise and approval from others. No one is oohing and aahing over the gorgeous flowers or fruit we're producing. It's the time when God's approval of us must be enough, and we earn His approval only through our acceptance of what Jesus did on our behalf at Calvary.

None of our works serve to gain His acceptance: "But we are all like an unclean thing, And all our righteousnesses are like filthy rags; We all fade as a leaf, And our iniquities, like the wind, Have taken us away" (Isaiah 64:6). Our experience in this fruitless season brings us to understand that without Him we are nothing, and this glimpse of our nothingness brings with it a greater understanding of the depth of His love for us.

Winter does its work in us; it leads us to an experience that changes us from the inside out. During these cold, hard days, our character is revealed, and we can deepen it. Helen Keller, who definitely had to endure her winter, wrote, "Character cannot be developed in ease and quiet. Only through experience of trial and suffering can the soul be strengthened, ambition inspired and success achieved."[2] Winter reveals the true nature of our character. There is an amazing experience awaiting you in stillness.

Be still, and know that I am God. (Psalm 46:10a)

"Be still" in Hebrew is *raphah*, a verb, an action word. Being still connotes a lack of action, but it is actually something we must take action to achieve. Raphah[3] means "to sink down, let drop, be disheartened, let go, be quiet, withdraw, or to be idle." This verse carries a promise; if we become still and let go of whatever is weighing us down and open up our hearts before Him; we will yada—experience God.

I am grateful to be past the uprooting and intense thirsting process. I have been replanted. I can take what I've learned from my winters and help others recognize theirs.

As a part of this replanting, God led me and my family to a new church home. It wasn't long after our replanting that I experienced another process of transplanting. As a church body, we entered a season of pruning, another one of those seasons that involves sharp tools and cutting. Within a two-week period, we went from a church staff of seven to a staff of two. Our worship pastor, senior pastor, youth worship leader, early childhood pastor, and church administrator were called out to different places by God's voice at the same time. It's a good thing we know we serve a God who won't abandon us.

As I was called upon to preach the main services the weekend before our beloved senior pastor left, I prayed. What does one say to a people who feel they've been somewhat ripped apart and abandoned? God revealed to me the season He was leading us out of and gave me a glimpse of the one soon to come. It's so important to seek out understanding. He commissions us to get understanding: "Wisdom is the principal thing; Therefore get wisdom. And in all your getting, get understanding" (Proverbs 4:7b).

Understanding changes everything. If we know what God is doing, it won't matter what lies Satan tries to plant as truth. We already know the truth and can spot the lies. The enemy is quick to accuse and spread rumors, doubt, and hopelessness the moment we enter our season change. "Discretion will preserve you; Understanding will keep you, To deliver you from the way of evil, From the man who speaks perverse things" (Proverbs 2:11–12). Understanding helps us guard our hearts and find peace in uncertain times: "Understanding is a wellspring of life to him who has it" (Proverbs 16:22).

God revealed to our church body that we had been in a dormant season. We had seen fewer numbers in our services and an incredible lack of volunteers to help carry out the missions we carried so strongly in our hearts. Some identified the season as one of apathy or discouragement. But God revealed the true condition of our church: we were in winter. He had to take us into a dormant season to prepare our hearts for the pruning process.

Our Gardener waits until winter to prune, and even though it pains Him to cut on His beloved tree, He cuts it, for He knows a lack of pruning will lead to unhealthy growth. During the pruning, He will remove branches that are beginning to grow in a different direction; He knows that if He doesn't, they will grow into the healthy branches and hinder growth on both sides. God revealed that there were some healthy branches in our body He was transplanting; He was preparing them to be ready for their next place.

He also removes unhealthy branches so they won't rob healthy branches of nutrients. The Gardener must quickly prune the branches He intends to graft onto other trees because they carry within them life for only a short time. The awesome thing about grafting is that the life the branches carry in them becomes one with the life in their next place, and together, they produce an entirely new fruit. God was going to take those precious branches from our church and graft them onto another, but He also promised to bring new branches into our body to produce new fruit in our community.

Pruning takes place right before spring and will allow a tree to flourish. I could see the signs of flourishing in our church as people were rising up to take the places of those who had departed, volunteering for positions we'd tried everything but bribery to fill. When we are waiting for spring, we can be confident it will bring with it amazing growth if we have allowed Him to prune us in the winter.

Our expectations are set by our understandings. If in our own understanding we believe we live in a perpetual season of harvest, we'll expect to see abundant fruit in others' lives as well as our own day in and day out. This of course is not truth and will lead to disappointment, frustration, and hopelessness. We must seek out His understanding.

> Trust in the LORD with all your heart, And lean not on your own understanding; In all your ways acknowledge Him, And He shall direct your paths. (Proverbs 3:5–6)

Have you ever found yourself in a weeding season? Not everyone in the country experiences weeding like we do in the Texas Panhandle. My hometown consists of very few trees, flat land as far as the eye can see, and plenty of cows. Our windy days have been known to blow over semis, carry trampolines from one yard to the next, and ensure that ladies of all ages keep ever mindful of their skirts.

Though rain is a treasure here, umbrellas are somewhat useless as the wind almost always turns them inside out. With these flat lands and crazy winds, weeds spread like wildfire; we have them in abundance. No matter how many hours we spend pulling them out of the hard ground, the wind will blow a whole new crop in by the end of the week. The problem with weeds is that they will quickly take over a yard, snuff out grass, and transform flowerbeds into weed gardens.

We have to get rid of the weeds before they consume our ground. Weeding is effective only when you pull out the weeds' roots. I've have played many games of tug-of-war with the ground;

it grips the roots while I pull the top of the weed. Many of my tug-of-war rounds have ended with the ground holding fast to the roots and me on my rear with a handful of weed tops. I know the roots are still there, thriving underground and will sprout up again in just days. I battle the same weeds, the same roots. If I could just pull out the roots, they'd never grow back.

We have to weed our hearts in much the same way. Though I feel I continually weed my heart, I remember when God led me into an intense weeding season just to pull one weed with very deep roots. My husband and I had just gotten married when he had to leave town for a sales seminar. I kissed him good-bye at the airport. My tears were flowing. That was probably to be expected; we knew we'd miss each other. But what wasn't expected was how many tears I was crying. By the time I got home, I was sobbing, grieving as if I'd never see him again, and I couldn't stop. I cried out to God to help me, to give me peace, to assure me I wasn't going crazy, but my tears intensified. At times, situations we go through might seem riduculous to others and maybe even to us, but God can use the smallest of things to do the biggest of works in us.

I couldn't get a grip on myself. I was sobbing at my kitchen table and couldn't understand why. I asked God to show me what was happening, and He gave me a vision. I saw my heart as a bountiful flowerbed with His huge but gentle hand hovering right over my heart, and in an instant He lifted His hand and a multitude of weeds shot out of the ground and blocked out all my flowers. Were the flowers gone? Had I lost everything I had worked so hard to grow in my life? There have been many times since that I wondered if my fruitfulness had been overtaken by weeds. At times like that, we can feel we're digressing, but I've come to learn that those are seasons of promotion. God is leading us into the next place, but before we can thrive there, He must remove some weeds lying beneath our surface. In His grace, He holds some weeds down until He sees we're ready to conquer them together.

The Holy Spirit brought revelation of that vision's meaning. For years, I had a gripping fear that someone I loved deeply would die. My husband worked in sales; I never knew when he'd be home. Many a night I had dinner ready only to have it sit for a couple of hours. He often had a late guest show up to test drive a few cars on their way home from work. During those nights, every siren I heard made my heart beat faster. I had recognized this fear, but it was a weed I had to continually tear off at the surface of my heart. I prayed, repented, and rebuked until I had peace, but the very next time a siren sounded, the battle would begin again. I had a deep-rooted fear. Praying it away wasn't enough. I had to find out where it was rooted.

My prayers led me to seek counsel; at times, we need the power of numbers to win the battle, and I was determined to win this one. As we prayed together, the Lord took me back to seventh grade, when my father was so paralyzed by fear that we weren't allowed to even go into the gated backyard of our house for fear something awful might happen. I was twelve, but I wasn't allowed to leave the house except for school. This root of fear had been passed down to me.

As crazy as it might sound, we inherit spiritual as well as physical attributes, good and bad. The apple doesn't fall far from the tree. The seeds sown in our foundation as children will sprout up later in life unless we do some weeding. Once I was able to find the root, I could pull it out. I repented that this fear had been allowed in my life, I forgave my father for cultivating this fear in my life, and I asked God to rip it out forever.

Sirens never again rocked me to my core. I walk in peace, not fear. He loved me so much that He wanted to deliver me from this paralyzing fear. How much time and energy had I spent worrying about what might happen? Once again, the enemy came to rob from my life. I hate weeding, but I'm so glad God led me into that season.

Some weeds are difficult to identify as weeds; when they first come out of the ground, they look like the flowers growing beside them. If we can recognize them early on, they're much easier to pull out. Many of our thoughts and battles are weeds. We think they are a part of who we are, but they were never meant to be in our lives. Trust the Gardener to help you identify and uproot the things in your life that aren't from Him. He paid the greatest price so you could live free of these life-smothering weeds.

What season do you find yourself in? Are you embracing it? If you don't recognize which season you're in, all you have to do is ask the Gardener where He has you right now, what season has He led you out of, and what season He is prepping you for. You have much to gain in your current season; you can miss out on some blessings if you don't decide to embrace this place and glean every treasure it holds.

Chapter Seven

The Octagon

> *When God has a new thing of a spiritual nature to bring into the experience of man, he begins with the senses. He takes man on the ground on which he finds him, and leads him through the senses to the higher things of reason, conscience, and communion with God.*[1]
> —Albert Barnes

I've always found it amusing that people pull out their best suits or evening gowns and get all glammed up to sit ringside and watch two men duke it out in a boxing ring. Of all the special occasions that call for such decorum, this almost seems ironic.

I must admit, though, I love to be on the couch and decked out in my sweats while rooting for the underdog with my husband. The MMA Octagon is our competition of choice. These athletes train and sweat it out for months, preparing for a win, watching and waiting to get that one shot or make that one move that grants them victory. Though I've never physically duked it out with anyone, I've endured many rounds in God's octagon and know that many more await me.

    Wrestling with God. Sounds sacrilegious, doesn't it? Who are we to think we're opponents worthy enough to step up against the One who created us out of dirt? Who are we to challenge Him and His ways? There are many "calls to the octagon" in the Bible, and my favorite is in Isaiah 1. God was speaking to Judah about the magnitude of their sin and the havoc it had wreaked on their city. He took seventeen verses to point out all the ways they'd failed to take care of themselves and their city, and then in one verse, He revealed hope, His heart, His way of fixing it: "Though your sins be like scarlet, they shall be white as snow, though they are red like crimson, they shall be as wool" (Isaiah 1:18b).

    But first, He extended an invitation to Isaiah: "Come now, and let us reason together" (Isaiah 1:18a).[2] The Hebrew for "reason" is *yakhach*,[3] "to dispute, argue, or to be convicted." He directs us to bring our reasoning, thoughts, wisdom, and perspective, and He'll bring His. And in His grace, He allows us to throw everything we have at Him, encouraging us to hold nothing back, and "leave it all in the cage" as they say in the world of MMA.

    My first "round" with God took place in my childhood. In my reasoning, I was a girl who did everything horribly wrong, a girl worthy of being rejected. My mother was an adamant churchgoer, one of those who did her best to be there every time the doors were opened with her three children in tow. While there, I'd hear that God loved me and thought I was special. I struggled to believe anyone could find any value in me, but He graciously led me into the cage, the octagon. I brought my reasoning, He brought His, and we wrestled until my faulty thinking was defeated. I stepped out of that round with changed reasoning. Not only did He not reject me, He also gave everything He had just so He could be in the same room with me.

    Before Jesus shed His blood for our sin, humanity couldn't be in the same room with the fullness of God's presence. This is another one of those hard-to-comprehend truths; His holiness cannot dwell with sin. Like wax to a flame is God's presence to sin, but He longed to walk with us again.

While the Israelites were wandering in the wilderness, God began His move into their midst. He gave Moses the blueprint to build His house, the tabernacle. God wanted a house built in the middle of His people, but He wanted it structured in such a way that unredeemed humanity would be protected from His radiance. The blueprint laid out measurements, the fabrics and metals to be used, and detailed instructions on how each piece was to be fashioned, formed, and joined together.

It contained a room to be called the Holy of Holies, where God would dwell. A veil draped from floor to ceiling, a cloth curtain that no one dared touch much less cross, was the divider between God and His people. Only the high priest was allowed in, and only on specific dates. Throughout the year, the high priest would venture beyond that curtain but only after very specific preparations were made and blood was shed to cover his sin and allow him access. If he didn't get it right, his unredeemed, sinful state would cost him his life.

God longed from the beginning of time to dwell with you and me, and at the moment Jesus surrendered His life on the cross, this veil literally ripped from top to bottom: "And Jesus cried out again with a loud voice, and yielded up His spirit. Then, behold, the veil of the temple was torn in two from top to bottom; and the earth quaked, and the rocks were split" (Matthew 27:50–51).

I'm sure the scientists and politicians of that day tried to explain away this supernatural act, but there was no denying God Himself had ripped the veil in half: "Never again will I have to measure My presence! Never again will My beloved have to stay in a room where I can't touch them." I've never been unable to touch my girls, but countless couples have had to experience a deep longing to hold their precious children but couldn't because the risk to their little ones' lives was too great. I can picture God in that place with every beat of His heart longing to reach out and touch the cheek of His child but knowing full well His touch would destroy His beloved. He just stands there staring and waiting.

It took a wrestling with my Creator to change my faulty way of thinking. And after our "reasoning together," I could actually believe I was loved by God and worthy of the greatest sacrifice of all, His Son. He took pity on me and delivered me; He even chose me as His bride! It wasn't an arranged marriage that you just show up to and hope she or he is cute and nice 'cause it's a done deal and whether you like him or her or not, he or she is going home with you for good. No. He chose you and me to be His bride for all eternity (Revelation 21:10). Though I stepped out of the cage changed, believing God loved me, I still had many more faulty reasonings that needed defeating.

When I was in high school, God began speaking to me about my future and the call He had placed on me. I have multiple prayer journals in which I wrote down the dreams and visions I've had. God has poured out prophetic words that others have spoken over me in different venues at different times, yet they all carry the same message—God has called me to preach, prophesy, sing, and write so even nations will hear the words He will speak through me and be changed (Joel 2:28).

But back then, I thought, *Ha ha, God! You must have the wrong person. I know You're big and You like to use people to do things on Earth, but I'm the least-qualified person. This whole speaking-to-crowds-thing? Do you remember my eighth-grade speech class? I've been rejected my whole life, who would want to hear anything I'd have to say? You want me to lead others? I'm really good at the whole "just tell me what to do and I'll do it" thing.*

You get the picture. I was quickly reminded by the Holy Spirit of Moses' similar conversation with God. Moses had been tending sheep for forty years, and one regular day on the job, he came across an intriguing sight—a bush on fire but not burning. Mesmerized, he probably stood still for a moment in awe; God has many creative ways of getting our attention. Moses finally decided to get closer to figure out what he was seeing. God revealed to Moses He would use him to deliver the Israelites from Pharaoh's wicked grip. Moses immediately responded with his faulty reasoning. And the wrestling match was on as they reasoned together (Exodus 3).

Jeremiah had an octagon moment with God as he wrestled with his call.

> Then the word of the LORD came to me, saying: "Before I formed you in the womb I knew you; before you were born I sanctified you; I ordained you a prophet to the nations." Then said I: "Ah, Lord GOD! Behold, I cannot speak, for I am a youth." But the LORD said to me: "Do not say, 'I am a youth, for you shall go to all to whom I send you, and whatever I command you, you shall speak. Do not be afraid of their faces, For I am with you to deliver you,' says the LORD." (Jeremiah 1:6–8)

To fulfill my purpose on Earth, I'd have to first step back into the cage and go another few rounds. My reasoning was that I was unqualified to be used by Him to do great things in this world. His reasoning was, "I choose the unqualified."

> For you see your calling, brethren, that not many are wise according to the flesh, not many mighty, not many noble, are called. But God has called the foolish things of this world to put to shame the things which are mighty; and the base things of the world and the things which are despised God has chosen, and the things which are not to bring to nothing, the things that are, that no flesh should glory in His presence. (1 Corinthians 1:26–29)

So once again I stepped out of the cage with transformed thinking; the fact I was such a mess and incredibly underqualified actually qualified me. In so many battles in the Old Testament, God ensured the odds were stacked against His people so He would get the glory and recognition for the win. He longs to reveal the power He pours out on our behalf.

It wasn't long before my next faulty reasoning came to the surface: *God doesn't need my help. After all, He's God and I'm just a person. He's all powerful, all knowing, and all present. He sees all and hears all.* I could picture the Fred Flintstone days with a gigantic brontosaurus lifting boulders and here comes a tiny gnat to lend a helping hand. What could God possible need from a person He couldn't just do Himself with one word? God's quick leading was, "Come, let's reason together again."

Have you heard that call? Did you step inside His ring? I can almost hear some of you longing to get in there and unleash all your pent-up anger. Forget the whole "call of God" thing; you just want your chance to cast all your abandoned moments, disappointments, and unanswered prayers at Him. Go! Take all your whys and where were Yous and give Him your best shot; give Him every single accusation you've been carrying. Don't hold back. What do you have to lose?

That backpack you carry through life must get heavy. There's no other way to get relief from that load than to set it down, open it, and empty it one rock at a time as you cast it back at the God who "let you down." Psalm 55:22 tells us to "cast our burdens on the LORD." The Hebrew definition for *burden* is "what is given by Providence." So hurl what you have been given by Providence at the One who gave it to you.

As I chose to accept His invitation once again, He gave me an analogy that changed my understanding of how and why God uses people. As a builder constructs a house by laying a foundation, erecting walls, installing utilities, he or she will complete the build by putting in place windows and doors that lock. When the job is done, he'll hand the keys to the homeowner and walk away. From this point on, If the builder wants back in, he'll have to get the keys from the homeowner.

Our Builder built us, and when He completed the job, He handed the keys over to us. He has to wait to enter our hearts, as we have the keys. He also built the Earth and gave man the keys.

> *And I will give you the keys of the kingdom of heaven, and whatever you bind on earth will be bound in heaven, and whatever you loose on earth will be loosed in heaven.* (Matthew 16:19)

> *Behold, I stand at the door and knock. If anyone hears My voice and opens the door, I will come in to him and dine with him, and he with Me.* (Revelation 3:20)

We have used our keys of authority over the Earth to allow much into our world that our loving Creator never meant to be a part of our lives. We, like Moses and his rod, have carried a power in our hands, in our hands, the keys that unlock Heaven on Earth. Without even realizing it, the daily decisions we've made as individuals, families, institutions, and governments have "loosed" things on this Earth and "bound" things in the spiritual realm. We've gone into various rooms called countries and cities and opened wide the windows for the enemy to flood in and wreak havoc.

I loved my moments as a children's pastor. While preparing for our Sunday morning lesson one morning, I read a passage of Scripture I've read countless times about the beginning in Genesis 1. I got to the part about the forbidden fruit and was blown away by the name of the tree whose fruit Adam and Eve were told not to eat, the Tree of the Knowledge of Good and Evil (Genesis 2:15–17). All parents desperately wish their children would never have to learn about the evil in the world. My youngest is about to start kindergarten. We've let her in on the evil of hunger and have shared with her about those who grow up without homes. We've gone through our clothes and toys and food and shared them with those in need. Some days, we pack extra lunches and drive around town asking God to show us someone who needs a sandwich.

We protect her from as much as we can while she has the privilege of innocence. We do our best to find that line of protecting and preparing her from and for this world. She and her big sister have such carefree giggles. Children are blessed with innocence; they don't bear the heaviness of heart that comes with the knowledge of evil. In the beginning, God didn't want His precious kids to ever have to know evil. By disobeying the one rule of the garden, eating of the Tree of Knowledge of Good and Evil, Adam and Eve used their key and opened the doors of Earth to Satan and all his evil.

It remains a mystery to me why God chose to run things that way, but He did. He chose to partner with humanity on Earth, to limit His place and power and position, to make Himself dependent on humanity when it came to the things of Earth. Read His own heart's cry: "So I sought for a man among them who would make a wall, and stand in the gap before Me on behalf of the land, that I should not destroy it; but I found no one" (Ezekiel 22:30).

He looks down on the Earth and thinks, *Please, someone, use the keys I gave you and unlock the door for Me so I can come in and rescue those who are held captive. I created the building, so I know how to reach the unreachable places, repair the foundation, and restore the worn-out utilities.* He needs us to hear Him, to know our callings, and to let Him wrestle faulty thinking out of us. We need to read His Word to understand the power and responsibility we hold in the keys He gave us.

I have two more rounds to share with you of my wrestlings with God. I share my stories to encourage you in yours. We've all been called to do amazing things as we accept our place next to

God. Without these changes in my thinking, I could never reach my destiny; my faulty beliefs would hinder my faith and ability to be used by Him to the fullest.

The next part of my journey consisted of God clearing up a little misconception I had about the "privilege" I'd received to do what He had been calling me to do. I looked at it as if I'd received an invitation from God that I could accept or decline. I was wrong. He took me back to a little story in the Bible about Jonah. It wasn't that I was considering declining God's invitation; my thinking that God's call was an invitation was the problem.

God gave Jonah the call to share His words with the people of Nineveh. I'm sure you're familiar with his declining of God's invitation. God sent him another one: "Now the LORD had prepared a great fish" (Jonah 1:7). Jonah's octagon experience didn't take place in a cage but in the belly of big fish, and once again, God told Jonah to go speak to Nineveh.

It must have been hard for Jonah. Nineveh was known as a city of sin, and God wanted him to tell its people to repent. What would you have said if you had been given that call? God's call on our lives is one of assignment, not invitation. This call had absolutely nothing to do with Jonah. It wasn't about his comfort zone, it wasn't about his reputation, it wasn't about his feelings—it was about a lost people separated from their God.

But it's not always the right time to go to a lost, sinning people and call them to repent. God had gone before Jonah and prepared their hearts to receive His Word. I can't even imagine an entire city putting on sackcloth and repenting before God today. The king of Nineveh decreed that everyone and their animals, from the least to the greatest, had to stop what they were doing, taste no food or water, get on their knees, acknowledge their sins, and turn from their wicked ways. Because Jonah fulfilled the call on his life, an entire city was redeemed and spared the disaster headed its way.

I'm confident that my next battle came as a result of the enemy launching some of his fiery darts into my core. "How dare you dream! You prideful, arrogant, selfish girl! Dreaming is wrong! How dare you desire to do great things! Just who do you think you are? God is disgusted with your wanting to do something big."

At times, the enemy's words have such power and force that they knock you off your feet. He'll work diligently to keep you from believing in your destiny for he knows the power of a destiny realized is the catapult of a destiny fulfilled. The enemy's plans can drive us into God's octagon. I got up off the floor running to Him to make sense of the chaos and confusion swirling inside me. I was in tears at the thought of having misheard Him and devastated to think He might have been disappointed in me. Some bouts take place simply by sobbing in His arms while His whisper rights our soul.

"My dear child, if you desire to do these things for self-gain, for others to know your name, to load your bank accounts, to disprove all who told you you couldn't, you dream for selfish gain. But dear one, if your heart beats like Mine, if you long to see the hurting laugh again, the lost find their way home, the lonely adopted, those that are bound be set free - then you're dreaming the dream I wove inside you. I created you to not only dream it but to live it."

What I walked away with from that encounter transformed my paradigm. He is the Creator of all things. I'm still amazed that fruit grows out of a tiny seed and that there are so many species of animals. His creativity is incomprehensible, yet His greatest invention is us.

When you think of all the greats—the greatest actor, athlete, musician, chef, artist—what are your expectations of them? If I see a movie that has Steven Spielberg's name on it, I expect it to be done well whether it's my kind of movie or not. Why? Because it's Steven Spielberg; look at all the amazing films he's produced. When you look at all the amazing things God has done—mountains, sunsets, waves, spectacular night skies, your best friend, a baby's tiny toes—what are your expectations of Him and what He can do? Why wouldn't you expect Him to be able to do "exceedingly abundantly above all that you could ask or think, according to His power that works in you" (Ephesians 3:20–21)? You are God's greatest masterpiece! He created you to do the most incredible, spectacular things; how insulting it must be to Him when we expect nothing much to come of His greatest creation.

I do now wholeheartedly believe God needs me and this Earth needs me to do my part, to run my leg of the race. But on my journey, I've seen so many great leaders start strong only to fall short before reaching the finish line. It seems that more fail to carry out their call than succeed. If God was ever to put me in a public ministry; if ever He was to use me to do big things, I'd have to be assured He'd help me finish strong.

I told God I'd rather never be in public ministry and live out my days longing for it than to start off in it and find my heart unable to handle the temptations of self-promotion. It's easy to cast judgment on those who walk in places where we've never stepped. We've all heard of people who held public ministries but ended them in a public fall. We all fall short; we all make choices we wish we hadn't. Those who live their lives in front of the world are no different. But those who are put in a position of leading others into spiritual truths know that with their falls, many, even thousands, are impacted by their landing. My heart grieves over all the wounded and dead who lie in the wake of public ministries gone bad. I wrestled with God for a long time in this. I could trust Him, but could I trust myself to be used by Him with a pure heart?

He assured me that He is a good trainer, the best at preparing us for what He calls us to do. He reminded me of my boot camp, one designed by Him specifically for me, and it has prepared me for my calling. His timing is perfect! If we wait for Him to lead us into our destiny, we can be assured He has gone before us and will come behind us (Isaiah 52:12).

Are you standing on the brink of your promised land? Do you fear what's ahead? It's wrong for us to refuse to take the land because of what we fear; that will turn our wilderness into a place of punishment. You might be peering upon giants with different characteristics than the ones I've seen on my land, but they are all destined to fall.

I've always been intrigued by Jacob's bout with God at the place he named Peniel (Genesis 32:24). When he was alone and empty-handed, "a Man wrestled with him until the break of day." It seems the best times to "bout" with God are when the sun goes down. The darkness pushes us toward Him. I don't imagine Jacob would have felt the need to wrestle if he hadn't been fearing for his life all alone in the dark. His encounter in God's octagon forced him to come to terms with his name and life he had lived fulfilling it.

"Jacob" in Hebrew means "heel grabber, deceiver." He deceived his own father into thinking he was Esau so he could have the blessing intended for his brother, the firstborn. In those days, your words meant everything; what was spoken came to pass. That was even true of the name you carried; the meaning of your name foreshadowed the life you would live. He was asked by his Opponent, "What is your name?" Ugh! That blow must have knocked the wind out of him. "I am a deceiver, God."

Bouts with God require us to reflect on the true condition of our hearts and see the places inside us that are not in right standing with His Word. If Jacob had quit at that point, ashamed or unwilling to face his past, he would have missed out on what God had next for him: "Your name shall no longer be called Jacob, but Israel; for you have struggled with God and with men, and have prevailed" (Genesis 32:28). The name "Israel" is translated as "Prince of God." God transformed Jacob from a deceiver, one who relied on himself to get ahead in this world, to a prince of God. From that moment on, he moved through life with God's power as an heir of the King of Kings. "Peniel" means "face of God." Jacob met face-to-face with God and exchanged the regrets of his past for an amazing future with all the power and provisions he would need to fulfill it.

Don't avoid God's octagon. He is the only opponent with Whom you're assured a loss and a win in the same round. What you lose pales in comparison to what you gain. God longs to replace the regret and pain of your past with an incredible future!

Chapter Eight

The Cloud

Eyes that look are common; eyes that see are rare.[1]
—J. Oswald Sanders

The sound of rain? There wasn't any thunder ringing from the sky or the sound of drops hitting the ground. It wasn't raining. It didn't even look like rain was possible—not a cloud in the sky, yet Elijah "heard the sound of rain" (1 Kings 18:41).

While I was visiting Israel, one of the places I was looking forward to touring most was Mount Carmel. When we arrived, the smell coming from nearby sulfur mines overwhelmed us. It's kind of ironic isn't it? The smell of sulfur at the place where the fiery battle of the gods took place thousands of years ago?

In Elijah's day, there were kings, rulers of nations seeking to snuff out believers. They sent terrorists to slaughter all the prophets of God; they decreed that belief in the God of Abraham, Isaac, and Jacob was a crime punishable by death. Does that sound familiar? Estimates are that between fifty-one and sixty countries around the world today have declared this belief in God punishable by imprisonment or death. Even in America, we are moving closer to the Bible being labeled a book filled with "hate crimes" and all who seek to live by it labeled as criminals. Wouldn't it be something if we had a Mount Carmel sequel today?

If you aren't familiar with the real-life story in 1 Kings 18, it's worth the read. Around 870 BC, King Ahab began his rule over Israel. He was one of many rulers to lead God's chosen people away from God. He launched his twenty-two-year reign by leading the nation to serve Baal, a god who demanded the blood of children. How sad that men choose to devote their lives to gods that seek only to steal, kill, and destroy over serving the God who came to bring life: "I have come that they may have life, and that they may have it more abundantly" (John 10:10a).

God sent Elijah to deliver the news to King Ahab that at the prophet's prayer there would be a drought in the land that would last for years. God wouldn't let one drop of dew fall on the land until Elijah proclaimed rain. Once again, we see the prophet of God carrying the burden of his people who were aimlessly straying from God, walking head-on into lives of misery.

Elijah longed to see the Israelites restored; he prayed for drought. I've heard many question his thinking. If he loved the Israelites, why would he ask God to make them thirsty? Movies throughout time have often depicted thirst by dropping a character alone in the desert with little water; even Daffy Duck had his turn. Daffy is in the desert, and we see the last drop drip from his canteen and the scorching sun become almost unbearable. His tongue hangs out, his strength fails, and before long, he's crawling on all fours through the hot sand; it isn't long before everything else is drowned out by thirst.

Thirst gets our attention; it causes our strength to fail and captivates our thoughts. We know there's only one way to look when we hit bottom. It's the heart of God to bring us back to the place of looking up before we destroy ourselves. It's only when we look up and seek His hand that He can rescue us. He intervenes only where He is invited. Elijah desperately wanted his nation, his people, to thirst so God could get their attention and rescue them.

But the moment it stopped raining, instead of believing God was powerful and meant what He said, King Ahab signed off on the murder of all the prophets of God. For the next three and a half years, believers had to hide or die, and the land dried up.

> *Elijah was a man with a nature like ours, and he prayed earnestly that it would not rain; and it did not rain on the land for three years and six months. (James 5:17)*

We read how God took care of His people during that time. One of the king's own men secretly provided a safe haven for a hundred prophets, and God commanded ravens to deliver food to Elijah. Can you picture this man sitting alone by the stream and waiting? He must have waited for a while, because the story tells us that he drank from that stream until it ran dry. While he waited, he was alone and vulnerable. He had no means of feeding himself, no one to keep him company.

I've read and heard this story preached more times than I can count, and it still baffles me that God told birds to take food to a lonely, hungry man. We have huge blackbirds in our area that just don't play nice with other birds. They chase the smaller birds away and hoard all the food they can find. It's a miracle that any bird could carry bread and meat without quickly devouring it for itself, and I have yet to meet a wild bird that doesn't quickly fly away when a person draws near. How refreshing to know that no matter how much terror reigns upon our land, our God will always take care of those who let Him.

> *The ravens brought him bread and meat in the morning, and bread and meat in the evening; and he drank from the brook. (1 Kings 17:6)*

When it was time for the drought to end, Elijah boldly approached King Ahab and gave him an order to gather all Israel along with the 850 false prophets (450 of Baal and 400 of Asherah) who polluted the people to the top of Mount Carmel. It seems thirst finally got the king's attention; he did as Elijah commanded, and the battle for fire from the heavens began.

I can't imagine what the people were thinking while they watched the 450 prophets of Baal cry out to their god and put their faith and hope to the ultimate test. This was the moment when a nation that had been led to serve and sacrifice and abandon all found out it had done so in vain. The combined prayers and morbid acts of worship were not enough to summon a response from Baal, so it was Elijah's turn. One man praying one prayer to the one true God. In an instant, fire fell from Heaven and consumed the dripping, wet altar with fire and quenched all doubt that He was God. Well, the story continues with the false prophets' executions, the end of a devastating drought, and a broken people returning to their loving God.

We love good stories, ones with obstacles and heroes and happy endings. As kids, we idolized those who laid it all on the line in self-sacrifice to save the day. We fashioned capes out of bath towels and emulated superhero cuffs with tin foil. We raced around the house, jumping from the couch to the chair, vanquishing imaginary bad guys while recusing damsels in distress. We were born in the image of God, the ultimate Rescuer. Even as adults, we secretly admire rescuers; we'd love to be them but don't really want to pay the price for the big muscles, selfless demeanor, and isolation that many times paves the way to heroism.

Elijah was most definitely a rescuer; he's listed in my hall of fame. I want to be like him. I want to hear God and see beyond the natural realm as one who walks in mega faith and is bold, brave, and confident and fears God above humanity. But I can't become any of these things without waiting upon the Lord and developing the discipline of perseverance.

Immediately following the rain of fire, they still desperately needed it to rain water upon the land, to end the devastating drought, and Elijah was appointed to pray it down. While it was still cloudless, Elijah admonished King Ahab to quickly eat, mount up, and get home because the rains were about to pour.

This is the most remarkable part of the story to me. He'd been commissioned by God to declare something to a king in front of a kingdom when there was no physical evidence to validate his proclamation. I often seek encouragement, signs to back up what I think I heard God say to me. On Mount Carmel, Elijah saw no signs of rain, but he'd heard His God speak. He told the king to hurry home, and the king listened.

But even as the king went on his way, Elijah had to wait and pray. That rain wouldn't come but at the word of this prophet (1 Kings 17:1). So what was he to do? There were no clouds in the sky. He did the only thing any of us should do when we need something we don't have; he got on his knees and prayed it in.

> Then Elijah said to Ahab, "Go up, eat and drink; for there is the sound of abundance of rain." So Ahab went up to eat and drink. And Elijah went up to the top of Carmel; then he bowed down on the ground, and put his face between his knees, and said to his servant, "Go up now, look toward the sea." So he went up and looked, and said, "There is nothing." And seven times he said, "Go again." Then it came to pass the seventh time, that he said, "There is a cloud, as small as a man's hand, rising out of the sea!" (1 Kings 18:41–44a)

This was a rampart moment for Elijah; he set himself on the ground, facedown before the Lord, waiting with full expectation that God would come through. He positioned himself in a place of waiting for the supernatural to change the natural. He refused to leave that posture until change came, until what God had promised was made manifest.

As is the case in many of these moments of supernatural intervention, we get a taste of the reality that all of us could possibly be used by God to do something big. In a similarly profound and powerful way, God could work through our prayers to change circumstances for the better. But we tend to look at the victory while overlooking the cost.

Yes, Elijah had heard God speak; rain was coming, and he was to spread the news to the very kingdom that sought to take his life. He heard and he went. He prayed fully confident that his prayers would change the skies; he refused to quit. How would this story have ended if Elijah hadn't learned to persevere? If he didn't know how to wait in faith until it was a completed work, he might have given up after the first six times of looking for the cloud. If he had placed himself anywhere else but on his rampart, he would have been easily defeated by doubt and impatience.

The moment the servant came back after looking for the seventh time, he reported a small cloud forming, and Elijah, in faith that this little puff in the sky was going to flood, got up and ran! There is running, and then there's "Elijah under the influence of Heaven" running. The Bible says that when Elijah stood, God touched him and he ran so fast he beat the king's chariot down the mountain.

I can picture this scene like a power-up on a video game or a nitrous boost in a drag race. One moment, the king is flying down the mountain with the fastest horse team pulling with all its might, and the next, Elijah blows by the chariot so fast the king probably doesn't even know what has just passed him (1 Kings 18:46).

I wonder what the servant was thinking. How foolish it must have looked for a man to run, believing a five-inch cloud was going to drench the ground. Elijah didn't care what men thought. This too was something waiting had developed inside him. How many people don't run into their destinies because they care too much about what others might think?

Perseverance is a rarity in our culture; so much has been given to us and given instantly. I barely remember the days of research papers without the web. I had to actually go to a library and find a physical book. If you've ever searched for one particular book in a library, you know how overwhelming that can be. In our library, there was a row of small, wooden boxes, stuffed full of index cards. To find a particular topic or author, you had to flip through each card until you found the one to point you in the right direction. Next to these boxes was a tub of scratch paper and tiny golf pencils for jotting down reference numbers. And that's when our search through the rows of books began. My searches usually ended with waiting my turn to ask one of the librarians to find a book for me, as I failed to find it myself. And after all that, I had to speed-read through page after page to find the answer or information I needed for my assignment.

How life has been changed by the Internet; all we have to do now is type in even a partial word and the computer does all the hard, time-consuming work for us. We don't even have to spell it right because Google understands what we meant to type, and we get frustrated if we have to wait a second for buffering. We can text our thoughts and questions to others immediately at any moment from anywhere and not have to wait until the next time we see them. I love our technology, and I love not having to wait, but there's something that waiting develops inside us that we lose when waiting is eliminated.

Merriam-Webster defines *persevere* as "to continue doing something or trying to do something even though it is difficult; to persist in an undertaking in spite of counterinfluences, opposition, or discouragement."[2] I've seen difficulties sway many from their dreams, but discouragement has taken out multitudes of dreamers. Mediocrity has become the norm because mediocrity is cheap and is easily acquired through the *drive-thru*. How many times have we heard the phrase "You get what you pay for"? I've heard it many times but always in terms of material purchases. However, the same rings true for mental, emotional, and spiritual purchases. Things we've waited for and have worked hard to achieve have a certain added value. If you pay for something with your time, it means much more to you and you're not quick to let it go.

There are many amazing stories about people who refused to give up and found great success through perseverance. Their stories show the fruit of perseverance and reveal that thing that is built-in to all of us, to get back up after being knocked down. In 1 John 5:4, we read, "For whatever is born of God overcomes the world. And this is the victory that has overcome the world—our faith." Some of these stories have been told numerous times, but I never tire of hearing them. These dreamers inspire me to never give up.

Walt Disney

Did you know this man was actually fired for "lack of imagination"? What if he'd chosen to believe the words of others rather than those in his heart? What would our lives be like today without the amazing works of Walt Disney? How many kids' rooms would be undecorated without the famous eared-hat? He worked hard to build his own company called Laugh-O-Gram Films in 1921 only to have to shut it down when his distributor went out of business. He spent his last pennies to move to Hollywood to present his cartoon of Oswald the Rabbit to Universal Studios. They patented his character and hired his artists out from under him.

He was told that Mickey Mouse and the Three Little Pigs would be complete failures. And it took sixteen years of his persevering to get permission from Pamela Travers to make her story of Mary Poppins come to life on film. I personally am glad he didn't get discouraged and give up on his dream.

Theodor Seuss Geisel

Here is a man who has written timeless children's books loved by children and adults alike, decade after decade. Dr. Seuss wrote over sixty kids' books that have sold over 222 million copies. These books have been translated into over fifteen languages.

I love the story of how his first book was created. He and his wife were sailing home from vacation when the rhythm of the ship's engines captured his attention and inspired him to write *And to Think That I Saw It on Mulberry Street*. He tried to get it published but was rejected more than twenty times. I wonder if any of those publishers regret that decision today. What if he'd never submitted it that last time? Can you imagine our world without *Green Eggs and Ham*?

President Abraham Lincoln

You've probably heard pieces of his story, but as I searched out his legacy, I found in this man an incredible overcomer. As a child, he lost his baby brother; his mother died when he was only nine. Later in life, his sister died giving birth. His first love died when he was twenty-two. Three of his children died before reaching adulthood. He was predominantly self-educated as his parents were most likely illiterate. Some reports say his neighbors remember him walking miles to borrow a book.

He ran for office but faced defeat six times. I'm amazed he was able to get out of bed any morning after all he'd endured. But he got up and changed the world.

Thomas Edison

Here's a man whose story of perseverance has been told repeatedly. I don't know how he would have fared if he'd been brought up in our instant-gratification world. As a young boy, he was misdiagnosed by his teacher as hyperactive, overly inquisitive, and mentally challenged, but his mother believed he had remarkable intelligence. He attributed her belief in him to be a major contributing factor of fashioning him into the man he became. He says of her, she "was the making of me ... she was always so true and so sure of me ... And always made me feel I had someone to live for and must not disappoint."

Thomas Edison earned 1,093 patents for his inventions, and not a one of them would have come about without perseverance. It took him thousands of attempts before he found the right materials and design for incandescent lightbulbs. He's recorded as having said he'd never failed; rather, he succeeded in finding out what didn't work, and that brought him closer to finding what did.

His success in inventing and doing all the hard work of getting patents led to great financial success. He invested in a large factory where more inventing could be done, but in December 1914, a huge fire destroyed his factory. He watched all his work, research, and earnings burn away, but he marveled at the incredible flames. He gathered his employees even as the firemen were fighting the fire and said, "We are rebuilding ... we can make capital out of disaster." He was quoted in the *New York Times* as saying, "Although I am over sixty-seven years old, I'll start all over again tomorrow." That's exactly what he did.

Some of his words resonate with his spirit of perseverance.

> Opportunity is missed by most people because it is dressed in overalls and looks like work.[3]

> Our greatest weakness lies in giving up. The most certain way to succeed is always to try just one more time.[4]

> Many of life's failures are people who did not realize how close they were to success when they gave up.[5]

What discouraging words hold enough power to keep you from stepping out in faith? What difficulty would hinder you from fulfilling your God-given dream? Are there words that echo in your mind that render you powerless to run? The tongue holds the power of life and death: "Death and life are in the power of the tongue, And those who love it will eat its fruit" (Proverbs 18:21). We have been given His authority to declare any destructive words spoken over us as powerless in our lives.

We are easy prey for discouragement. We read of the incredible battles in the Old Testament in which people faced overwhelming odds. They either had to fight physical battles with swords and sweat or be enslaved or destroyed. Most of us fight battles that at times make us feel we're facing overwhelming odds, but I've yet to meet anyone who wields a sword. I almost think it's easier to choose to fight a physical battle *or* die than it is to choose to fight a mental battle *or* settle for mediocrity. We love movies in which people living normal lives suddenly find themselves having to fight and run to survive. They almost always find themselves doing things they would never have done were it not for the dire circumstances forced on them; they discover there's more inside of them than they realized. They're more capable of hunting, hiding, running, fighting, and problem solving than they imagined. Because the cost of not fighting, hunting, and hiding is more than they're willing to pay, they dig deeper than they've ever dug and out of sheer motivation to survive, they fight!

For those of us not living in physical war zones, we have battles launched at our minds, but the cost to our lives is not enough for us to dig deep and fight. We are bombed by fear, insecurity, anxiety, doubt, hopelessness, depression, procrastination, apathy, compromise, and fatigue. At times, these can feel overwhelming; we try to think positive thoughts and whisper a prayer, but when that doesn't work fast enough, we often settle and give in to the thought that the next level of faith walking or maturity or breakthrough really isn't worth it.

I love what a dear friend had to say when her daughter chose to wear last year's Easter dress with this year's snow boots and a baseball cap to play her instrument at the spring recital: "I'm choosing my battles." What or who is worth your fight? What have you given up on because it wasn't worth your effort to persevere?

Character is not free, nor is it for sale at any local market. Our culture has made a mockery of character. The most popular movies and television series of our day serve as mirrors that reflect what we hunger for as a society; we feed on an entertainment diet of junk food. Series that aren't cancelled after the first few weeks of airing create places the majority of us want to dive into every week.

If we reflect on the role models of yesterday, we see men and women of integrity, people who stood for something and paid a great price for their success. They inspired many to keep growing. Many of our role models today—musicians, actors, athletes, politicians among them—are all over the news but not for the way they're changing the world for the better. It actually seems that more times than not, those in the limelight who stand up for something pay a great price for it. Actors are denied movie roles; athletes are criticized for having character; their refusal to compromise is not admired but ridiculed.

God wants us to persevere. Romans 5:3–5 reads,

> And not only that, but we also glory in tribulations, knowing that tribulation produces perseverance; and perseverance, character; and character, hope. Now hope does not disappoint, because the love of God has been poured out in our hearts by the Holy Spirit who was given to us.

I love the way it is worded in *The Message* version.

> There's more to come: We continue to shout our praise even when we're hemmed in with troubles,

> because we know how troubles can develop passionate patience in us, and how that patience in turn forges the tempered steel of virtue, keeping us alert for whatever God will do next. In alert expectancy such as this, we're never left feeling shortchanged. Quite the contrary—we can't round up enough containers to hold everything God generously pours into our lives through the Holy Spirit! (Romans 5:3–5)[6]

Waiting can fashion character and hope in us. The word translated as *character* in this passage in Greek is *dokime*, "proof of genuineness; approval through testing, something that is tested and found true."[7] This same word has been used of testing metals. There are a variety of methods used to determine a metal's makeup, durability, and ability to tolerate high temperatures and stress. Metals proven to be durable are used to perform incredible tasks, while the others are rejected.

God tests us to reveal to us what we're made of and what we can and can't handle. As our weaknesses are revealed, He offers to turn our weak areas into areas of our greatest strengths. If we allow Him to do His work in us, we can step off our rampart—tested and approved—to be used by Him for incredible tasks.

It is in our waiting, that we are transformed more into His image. He deepens our character so that we're better equipped to stand and to run. When we have God-fashioned character, our integrity is not changed in the midst of changing circumstances; it's is genuine and true; it can pass the tests of life, because it's has already been tested, and approved by God Himself.

The time we spend waiting on our ramparts enables us to stand when those around us bow, and it cultivates an environment in our hearts in which hope can grow and thrive. This word *hope* in Greek is *elpis*, "to anticipate or expect something as a sure thing."[8] Is this not the perfect picture of what Elijah did? He expected the rain as a sure thing. It didn't matter that he didn't see it the first six times he looked, and it didn't matter that the seventh time he looked, the cloud he prayed so hard to see was only the size of a fist. He walked in *elpis*, assured his God was everything He proclaimed to be and would do everything He said He would.

If you are called to break through, if you are called to be used by God, if you were created and placed on Earth for a purpose, if you will "outlive" your life and leave a legacy that impacts generations, you'll have to walk the road of character building. God will direct you to take the path less traveled. He will allow your boot camp (your circumstances) to produce perseverance, character, and hope.

When was the last time you heard God speak a word to you? There are times He speaks to me but I don't recognize His still, small voice. I dismiss the Holy Spirit's voice as my own thoughts. I believe He speaks to us all the time but we often don't hear or recognize Him. His voice is drowned out by the constant sound bed we stream into our daily world, or we hear Him and we doubt it's His voice. We must first recognize that voice, and to do that, we have to spend time with Him. We can familiarize ourselves with His voice by reading His Word and spending time in prayer and listening in stillness: "Be still, and know that I am God" (Psalm 46:10a).

In 1 Kings 18, one man knew and recognized God's voice. He held on tight to the Word of the Lord. If he hadn't been seeking God, it would have just been a tiny little cloud he saw. Maybe you finally see a cloud but it's only the size of a fist. Is your soul disappointed at the sight? "Is this it? God, is this what I've been waiting for?" We don't know what went on in Elijah's servant's mind, but Elijah recognized the cloud for what it was. He saw with spiritual eyes. He knew that tiny cloud was the long-awaited promise of God, and he couldn't run fast enough.

I love the way this Mount Carmel experience reveals how the fires of the wait sharpen the sword of faith. Elijah had to persevere in prayer and faith. He had heard God say that rain was coming. He took God at His Word, but that was all he had to hold onto during his wait. The wait is where our faith is tested most. We long and pray for greater faith, but we doubt God's love for us when we have to wait. But maybe the wait is His answer to our prayers. What clouds of promise or change are awaiting your prayer of breakthrough? Are you tired and weary of the drought in your land?

Maybe you've heard a promise from God; maybe you've heard His voice and believe His words of the impossible. You maybe have even already spoken them out in faith but have yet to see the cloud form. Don't quit. Don't stop praying. Don't give up on Him. Don't believe the lie that He has let you down. Go look again and again and then again, and when you see a tiny cloud forming, let hope trickle in and give you the strength to run into your breakthrough.

Chapter Nine

The Plunder

*There are far, far better things ahead
than any we leave behind.*[1]
—C. S. Lewis

Plunder is what comes after the war is over and the battle is won. Each battle has its own reward at the end for the taking. Some battles leave us depleted, while others leave our pockets full of the enemy's treasure. Once we make it through to the end, we're generally worse for the wear, fatigued, bruised, and bloodied. All battles carry a price. So before we step out onto the battlefield, we ask, "What's it going to cost me? What's in it for me? Why would I risk anything or even everything for this thing that is being asked of me?" And the Bible warns us to consider the cost before saying yes.

> And whoever does not bear his cross and come after Me cannot be My disciple. For which of you, intending to build a tower, does not sit down first and count the cost, whether he has enough to

> finish it—lest, after he has laid the foundation, and is not able to finish, all who see it begin to mock him, saying, 'This man began to build and was not able to finish'? Or what king, going to make war against another king, does not sit down first and consider whether he is able with ten thousand to meet him who comes against him with twenty thousand? (Luke 14:27–31)

When we enter the battlefield, we leave the comforts of home, family, and friends behind for a time. We push our minds and bodies to extremes, keep our emotions at bay, and put our lives on the line. There is glory in a soldier's story, but the glory in his win doesn't come without pain. So the question comes, "Is it worth it?" As we consider the cost and worth of the battle, we should include the plunder awaiting us at the end; many times, it's the reason we find the courage and strength to charge onto the field.

So what does battling and plunder have to do with the rampart in our own lives? Waiting. Persevering. Surrendering. Stepping into God's Octagon. Shifting Viewpoints. Identifying and Embracing a Season. Becoming Vulnerable. Dreaming Big. All these are fields of battle we must *choose* to step into. We should consider what it will cost us and what we'll gain before we say yes or no.

Countless stories tell of soldiers and their incredible battles; the men and women involved in them had to ask and answer these questions before they got their win. If we could just peek ahead and see the outcome, it would certainly make our answering easier. The incredible thing about walking with God is that He sees ahead always; He's omnipresent. He's not limited to parameters of time; He is in all time periods simultaneously. He already knows what our enemy looks like, how strong he will be, the weapons he will bring, and the outcome. There is a divine timing to battling, and God always gives wise counsel. He even gives detailed strategy for winning the fight.

Throughout the Old Testament, leaders sought the Lord before going into battle as they considered the cost. King David, who faced many battles, knew to seek God's counsel before marching against the enemy.

> Then the Philistines went up once again and deployed themselves in the Valley of Rephaim. Therefore David inquired of the Lord, and He said, 'You shall not go up; circle around behind them, and come upon them in front of the mulberry trees. And it shall be, when you hear the sound of marching in the tops of the mulberry trees, then you shall advance quickly. For then the Lord will go out before you to strike the camp of the Philistines.' And David did so, as the Lord commanded him; and he drove back the Philistines from Geba as far as Gezer. (2 Samuel 5:22–25)

Moses weighed these questions as he stood barefoot in front of the burning bush. Would he say yes to going head-to-head with Pharaoh? What would that cost him? He was on Egypt's most-wanted posters for murder. It must have been painful to go back to the place where he once lived as royalty after having fled forty years earlier. He left his home, his friends, his family, and his set future behind. Those he would be fighting for most likely would despise him for his upbringing. He was new to this trusting God stuff. And his adoptive brother would be on the opposite end of the battlefield. What would his wife's family say to his crazy notion of going back to Egypt? What weapon did he have that could compete with those in Pharaoh's arsenal? All he had was a stick and His God's assurance, but he said yes.

God saw ahead and told him victory would come and with it the plunder of Egypt.

> So I will stretch out My hand and strike Egypt with all My wonders which I will do in its midst; and after that he will let you go. And I will give this people favor in the sight of the Egyptians; and it shall be, when you go, that you shall not go empty-handed. But every woman shall ask of her neighbor, namely, of her who dwells near her house, articles of silver, articles of gold, and clothing; and you shall put them on your sons and on your daughters. So you shall plunder the Egyptians. (Exodus 3:20–22)

This plunder must have been somewhat of a nuisance. They went out of Egypt on foot, which means they had to carry anything they took with them for miles and miles over rough terrain. What good would gold and clothing be in the desert anyway? Sometimes, the plunder we find doesn't look like much, but many times, it's meant for a later season. Isn't it just like God to use our past wins to build our futures? The Israelites couldn't eat gold on their journey, but God wanted to give it to them because He had great intentions for it, in their future.

Sometime after the Red Sea crossing and the pillars of fire and cloud, in the middle of their wilderness experience, God revealed His plan for all that plunder. The Egyptians' gold, jewels, and fabric were to be used to build the tabernacle. Pharaoh sought to snuff out the Israelites' belief in God, but ironically, his wealth became the materials used to bring God's presence among the people. God was ready to dwell on Earth in the midst of His people again. He has always longed to be in their midst; He wanted to walk with them since the day He fashioned them out of dirt. He had been separated from humanity after the fall in the garden of Eden, but

He had a plan to once again be in their midst. His plan included taking what the enemy meant for harm and using it for good.

> *And we know that all things work together for good to those who love God, to those who are the called according to His purpose.* (Romans 8:28)

I love the story of Joseph and his brothers. His was a life that demonstrated trusting in God despite our circumstances. His battlefield was one of forgiveness and integrity in the midst of injustice. He had eleven brothers and a sister, but he was the favorite. Being second to last in line as the eleventh son, he didn't stand to gain much in the way of inheritance. And as my cousins and I used to joke about being stuck at the kids' table until we had grandchildren; Joseph would most likely have never been bumped up to the adult table at holiday meals.

But when he was seventeen, God began to speak his destiny to him in his dreams and revealed he would one day become a leader ruling over his family, and they despised him for it. In those days, they understood the significance of God-breathed dreams, and his older brothers couldn't tolerate the thought of their favored, younger brother being placed above them. If they were jealous before, that news put them over the top. They began to despise Joseph, and the resentment that festered in their hearts became hatred for him.

One day while the brothers were out taking care of the flock, they saw Joseph approaching, and the final argument over how to get rid of him began. They beat him, stripped off his colorful coat, and tossed him into a pit. They debated killing him or just abandoning him there. I love how God used these horrible intentions to direct Joseph's path. They saw a caravan of slave traders passing by, and dollar signs flashed in their minds. They pulled Joseph out of the hole—he was bleeding, dirty, and half-naked—and they sold him as a slave.

This is just one of many testimonies in the Word that show us that the enemy won't hinder God's plans for us as long as we walk with Him. The brothers told their father he had been killed by wild animals and made up evidence to confirm their lie and cover their sin.

Joseph's journey out of his father's favored eyes into slavery soon led to his being falsely accused and imprisoned for a crime he had refused to commit. There is much more detail to his amazing story in Genesis 37–50, but to sum it up, he held tight to his dream, forgave his brothers, denied grief lordship over his life, and become the best slave and prisoner the Egyptians had ever seen. His integrity and relationship with God led to his promotions, and he was eventually named second in command over all Egypt, second only to Pharaoh.

God used him and his position to save the people from a severe famine that was to hit seven years down the road. When the famine struck, his brothers had to go to Egypt for food, and it was up to Joseph to provide it for them. He could have said, "I told you so! You deserve to starve for what you did to me. Guards, arrest these men and let them see what prison's like!" But again, he chose the way of forgiveness, integrity, and righteousness.

> Joseph said to them, "Do not be afraid, for am I in the place of God? But as for you, you meant evil against me; but God meant it for good, in order to bring it about as it is this day, to save many people alive." (Genesis 50:19–20)

Joseph's yes and faithfulness to God in his circumstances brought him plunder in the form of a dream come true, a heart free from the grip of bitterness, abundant favor and riches in the land in which he was once a slave, and the opportunity to rescue a generation from starvation.

In reading his story, I find myself asking what I would have done in his shoes? How am I dealing with the betrayals and unjust moments of my life? Am I quick to be the very best at whatever job is in front of me? Do I choose, daily, to trust God even when my dream seems impossible and He seems unfaithful, or life seems unfair? Have I forgiven those who have wronged me?

Our yes and our plunder are not just for us. God uses the plunder from our bondages, battles, waits, winters, and perseverance to bring us closer to Him. Yet through these, He comes into our midst, builds a bridge through us, and allows our lives to be used to draw others to Him.

Esther's story is one of these incredible bridges; she was another prisoner of war granted favor by an enemy king. She was forced into the harem of a king who burned cities and took people as plunder. This orphan girl became the best candidate for the next queen of Persia. Sometime after her coronation, she learned that one of the governing leaders had issued a decree to annihilate her people, the Jews. They were to be destroyed, young and old, for their faith. God asked her what her answer would be. Would she violate the rule of the king and invite herself into his chambers? Would she reveal herself to be a Jew? Would she ask the king to overturn the order to murder all Jews? She had to weigh the cost; if she said yes, she might be sentenced to death. If she said no, her people would perish. While considering her answer, she received this counsel.

> For if you remain completely silent at this time, relief and deliverance will arise for the Jews from another place, but you and your father's house will perish. Yet who knows whether you have come to the kingdom for such a time as this? (Esther 4:14)

She realized in her valley of decision that her position had been granted to her not simply for her pleasure but to save a generation. I find myself prayerfully wishing that those in positions of authority today recognize their positions haven't been given to them solely for their own success. God gives leadership roles to men and women for the sake of the people they lead. Queen Esther heard the words of her mentor and immediately said yes.

> Then Esther told them to reply to Mordecai: "Go, gather all the Jews who are present in Shushan, and fast for me; neither eat nor drink for three days, night or day. My maids and I will fast likewise. And so I will go to the king, which is against the law; and if I perish, I perish!" (Esther 4:15–16)

Esther took the battlefield and plundered the enemy of her people. What did she gain? Her plunder came in form of public proclamation that she was highly favored in the eyes of King Ahasuerus. Her story in the Bible inspires all who read it. Her bravery and obedience is remembered every year during the Feast of Purim; God used her to deliver His people. Her yes gave her people favor with their enemy king. The Jews were spared and strengthened as part of her reward. And she got to bring the one who sought to destroy her people to justice.

All these Bible stories seem so distant. We don't know much of kings and kingdoms here in America. We've been spared captivity in other nations. Though the times are dramatically changing, I can more easily relate with these individuals who looked over a land and a people they loved being threatened for their faith. At this point, at least on American soil, our battlefields look different and the cost might not be that of our physical lives thanks to our soldiers. Their yeses and sacrifices have spared us captivity and devastation. I can't put into words my gratitude for their answering the call to fight on our behalf and keep us safe.

Spiritual warriors have poured out their lives in prayer and spiritual warfare so we could find and dwell in hope and freedom.

It's humbling to think that our spiritual yeses could be used to do the same for others. Our battles often take place in our hearts and minds—in the spiritual realm.

God speaks to me through everyday things, and sometimes, He lays it upon my heart to share these thoughts with others. At times, I sense I'm supposed to post my thoughts on social media, and I've wrestled with that. *Maybe they only serve to inspire me. No one really likes to read long posts. Social media is not the place to be preachy.* But then, the pressing of the Holy Spirit upon my heart to post moves over me again, and so I post.

God knows what others around us are battling, and the encouragement they need might be found in sharing what He is speaking to our hearts. This alone is a simple battleground. To post or not to post something, to speak a word to a friend, to approach the stranger behind us at the grocery store, to ask our waiters and waitresses if they have prayer requests—these are just a few examples of God asking us to step out. It will cost us vulnerability and boldness. It might cost us time that we don't have. We might encounter a question we don't know the answer to or lose a Facebook friend. We don't always know why He moves in our hearts to speak something out we might think is insignificant, but will we say yes?

One of my Facebook posts came to me in the middle of the night after I'd run my first 5K. A few months before the race, my sister asked if I would run it with her. I didn't know what to expect, but since it was for a good cause and would be a great challenge to do together, we signed up and decided to register my girls to run too.

The day of the race came; we got up bright and early after a very late night. I could hear my husband's words of warning, echoing in the back of my mind as we lined up. "Are you sure the girls are going to do it and you won't be carrying them through the whole race?" I had one of those moments of God speaking to me in the daily things halfway through this race. Here's the post I later shared.

The Stroller vs. The Scraped Knee

As I started the run this weekend, I was quite unsure how my five-year-old would cope. She sprinted out of the starting line with a huge smile that faded fast into tears as she tripped and scraped her knee.

I just happened to have Band-Aids ready for such a moment, but they didn't make it all better. And so I carried her piggyback uphill for a ways. Then it was time, and I gave her the "You're a big girl, and it might hurt a little, but you can do this" talk, and she did it! She jogged with me the rest of the way, racing to get her medal at the finish line!

Halfway through, I noticed a little guy riding through the race in his stroller. I could "hear" the countless times people say they missed those days of being carried through life.

Though the life of being carried is a scrape-free one, it's also one without medals and accomplishments. I feel compelled to share this for those who are hearing the Lord say, "It's time to run!"

If you could have seen the look on Maddy Kate's face when she crossed that finish; the joy she felt in running and overcoming was far greater than the already-forgotten pain of her fall.

We can't let the fear of falling keep us from reaching our medals!

#RunIntoYourCalling

I share this with you to encourage you to add to your cost counting the plunder of accomplishment. Whatever God is asking you to do in this season of your life, know that remaining where you are might feel safe and comfortable, but it's a "stroller" in your life. He will always challenge you to grow to the next level. His best for each of us is to run through life, not to be carried. If He's asking you to run and you say no, you'll miss out on the confidence and joy that comes with crossing the finish line.

The Israelites received their medal, the Promised Land. The place where their enemy taunted them and their God, is the very place that became the fulfillment of His incredible promises. This was the place where they bore their best fruit, the land where they grew deep roots and birthed their legacy. The Promised Land was the land generations would rise up out of and accomplish God-breathed dreams.

But before they could do any of these incredible things, they had to slay giants. Each of us has a promised land awaiting us, a place of fruitfulness and legacy, ground that is ours for the taking but is currently occupied by giants. The enemy is no pushover. He won't allow you to breeze into your promised land uncontested. God is also no pushover; He will give you the strategy and the strength, and the win, if you seek His face.

There is plunder in battles we choose as well as in battles that choose us. It's up to us to take it or walk away from it. Sometimes, I've had to ask God to show me the plunder I could glean from a tough season I'd just endured. Plunder can be hard to see when we're exhausted and wounded. It doesn't always look like something we'd find in a treasure chest.

One of these hard-to-identify plunders is wisdom. We learn through the fight; we learn the ways of war that no lecture, training, or book could teach us. Experience is a teacher of a different sort. We learn the value of hearing His voice and seeking His counsel. Battles reveal the truth that we can't successfully rely on our own understanding. My fights have taught me much about my God as well as my enemy and his ways. After my past encounters with him, I'm better prepared to face him next time he shows up. I'm also able to help others recognize some of the enemy's tactics in the battles they're facing.

Gratitude is another treasure gleaned from the battlefield. When we're faced with losing everything, we redefine what really carries value in our hearts. You've probably heard it said that a person who has never been sick doesn't appreciate healing as much as the one who desperately needed it does. Peace is most enjoyed by those who have walked outside of it; freedom is truly understood by those who have felt the chains of bondage. Battles reveal all we have been given and the things we often take for granted.

Not all plunder is good. We must be wary of the enemy's enticement of cursed plunder. Revenge, judgment, bitterness, and pride might be there for the taking, and these sometimes spark a battle in themselves as we fight to leave them behind. Pride is one of the toughest to leave when we walk off a battlefield as conquerors. It's in our nature as human beings to forget what God has done for us. Staying humble is an attitude we have to adopt daily. If we aren't intentional in guarding our hearts against it, pride will take over and consume us fast.

When others see the incredible treasures we carry, it's easy for us to take the credit for the win. I pray one prayer regularly as a part of my intentional seeking to live in humility rather than pride: "Lord, I ask to be a bush that burns so hot that it draws others in, but let those who gather around not see the bush, only the Fire." I want those around me to realize I'm nothing but a carrier of His amazing life and power; I'm just the bush; He's the Fire. Without Him, I am nothing, but with Him, nothing is impossible.

Battles usually carry within them loss in one form or another. If you've lost much because someone has taken it from you or you've squandered it like the Prodigal Son; God is in the restoration business. He can always restore more than what was lost or stolen. But loss carries with it the cursed plunder of regret; we must find a way to leave that behind, not even pick it up. Regret will steal from us, drain our joy and peace, and hold us back from the great things awaiting us. We must drop it at the feet of Jesus. When I can't let go of something bad, I ask Him to wash it away with His river of life and peace. It's incredible what His river can wash away.

God is a Warrior, and we were created in His image; we're warriors too. "The Lord is a man of war; the Lord is His name" (Exodus 15:3). This Earth is a battlefield, and our enemy is not weak or ignorant of battle tactics. He's skilled, cunning, stealthy, and out for the kill. He's won many battles, but it's written that he'll lose the war. On his way to defeat, I want to inflict as much damage on his kingdom as I can. I seek to pour my life out and encourage others to do the same. We weren't created to live lives sitting down. We were born to run; to shine God's light into the dark places of our world. We are called to be carriers of His living water to those who are dirty, hurting, and thirsty.

The only way to run and keep running is to say yes to our rampart experiences He is calling us to share with Him. The Bible tells us repeatedly that God is good all the time and always has our best interest in mind. If this is true, we can be confident that any battlefield He asks us to take will have incredible plunder awaiting us. As you consider the cost, know that your yes carries abundant life not only for yourself but for others as well—people you know and some you've yet to meet.

Conclusion

We've journeyed through various ways we find ourselves at the bottom rung of the stairway leading to the rampart. It is my heart and prayer that you're encouraged and challenged to make the climb. My heart for sharing these encounters with you is to help you overcome whatever is standing in your way. You were created in His image with an incredible destiny.

He is good, faithful, trustworthy, and loving. He is always there, and He delights in you. He not only calls you by name; He counts the hairs on your head.

If He is calling you to meet face-to-face with Him, don't miss this incredible moment. My prayer is that you find the courage and strength to climb atop your rampart and peer into the distance with unwavering expectation that He will come and perform the impossible in your heart when He meets and reasons with you face-to-face.

Notes

Chapter 1: The Wait
1. A. W. Tozer, *The Root of the Righteous* (Chicago: Moody Publishers, 1955, 1986).
2. *The Living Bible*, copyright © 1971 by Tyndale House Foundation. Used by permission of Tyndale House Publishers, Carol Stream, IL. All rights reserved. The Living Bible, TLB, and the The Living Bible logo are registered trademarks of Tyndale House Publishers.
3. *Merriam-Webster OnLine*, s.v. "rampart," http://www.merriam-webster.com/dictionary/rampart.
4. James Strong, *The New Exhaustive Strong's Numbers and Concordance with Expanded Greek-Hebrew Dictionary* (Biblesoft and International Bible Translators, 1994).

Chaapter 2: The Deal
1. Jeanne Mayo, *JEANNEISMS: Short Thoughts That Echo Big Meaning* (Atlanta: A Youth Leader's Coach Publication, 2011).
2. *Biblesoft's New Exhaustive Strong's Numbers and Concordance with Expanded Greek-Hebrew Dictionary* (Biblesoft and International Bible Translators, 1994).
3. Ibid.
4. Corrie Ten Boom, *The Hiding Place* (New York: Bantam; published by arrangement Fleming H. Revell Company, 1971, 1974).

Chapter 3: The View
1. Billy Graham, *Unto the Hills: A Daily Devotional* (Nashville, TN: Thomas Nelson, 1986, 1996, 2010).
2. Benjamin B. Warfield, "Some Thoughts on Predestination," in *The Christian Workers Magazine*, volume 17 (Chicago: Moody Bible Institute, 1916).

Chapter 4: The Dream
1. Dutch Sheets, *Dream Discovering God's Purpose for Your Life* (Minneapolis: Bethany House, 2012).
2. Bruce Wilkinson with David and Heather Kopp, *The Dream Giver* (Colorado Springs: Multnomah Books, 2003).
3. Andy Stanley, *Visioneering: God's Blueprint for Developing and Maintaining Vision* (Colorado Springs: Multnomah Books, 1999).

Chapter 5: The Rod
1. Charles Spurgeon, *Penny Pulpits*, 1865; www.godwithyou.org/charles-spurgeon-quotes-on-suffering.htm.
2. *Biblesoft's New Exhaustive Strong's Numbers and Concordance with Expanded Greek-Hebrew Dictionary* (Biblesoft and International Bible Translators, 1994).

Chapter 6: The Season
1. Lewis Carroll, *Alice's Adventures in Wonderland & Through the Looking Glass* (UK: Mass Market Paperback: Penguin [USA], 1871, 2000).
2. http://www.movemequotes.com/top-11-helen-keller-quotes/.
3. *Biblesoft's New Exhaustive Strong's Numbers and Concordance with Expanded Greek-Hebrew Dictionary* (Biblesoft and International Bible Translators, 1994).

Chapter 7: The Octagon
1. Albert Barnes, *Albert Barnes' Notes on Genesis 32:37*, "Notes on the Bible by Albert Barnes" (text courtesy of internet sacred texts archive, www.BibleHub.com, 1834).
2. *Biblesoft's New Exhaustive Strong's Numbers and Concordance with Expanded Greek-Hebrew Dictionary* (Biblesoft and International Bible Translators, 1994).
3. Ibid.

Chapter 8: The Cloud
1. J. Oswald Sander, *Spiritual Leadership: A Commitment to Excellence for Every Believer* (Chicago: Moody Bible Institute, 1967, 1980, 1994).
2. http://www.merriam-webster.com/dictionary/.
3. Edison Innovation Foundation, http://www.thomasedison.org/index.php/education/edison-quotes/.

4. Thomas A. Edison. BrainyQuote.com, Xplore, 2015,. http://www.brainyquote.com/quotes/quotes/t/thomasaed149049.html; accessed September 6, 2015.
5. Ibid.
6. Scripture taken from *The Message*, copyright © 1993, 1994, 1995, 1996, 2000, 2001, 2002. Used by permission of NavPress Publishing.
7. *Biblesoft's New Exhaustive Strong's Numbers and Concordance with Expanded Greek-Hebrew Dictionary* (Biblesoft and International Bible Translators, 1994).
8. Ibid.

Chapter 9: The Plunder
1. C. S. Lewis, *The Collected Letters of C. S. Lewis: Narnia, Cambridge, and Joy 1950–1963* (London: Harper Collins, 2006).

Made in the USA
San Bernardino, CA
20 January 2016